COMMON LAW: THE INTRODUCTION

AUSTRALIA
Law Book Co.
Sydney

CANADA and USA
Carswell
Toronto

HONG KONG
Sweet & Maxwell Asia

NEW ZEALAND
Brookers
Wellington

SINGAPORE and MALAYSIA
Sweet & Maxwell Asia
Singapore and Kuala Lumpur

COMMONHOLD LAW: THE INTRODUCTION

Trevor M. Aldridge
M.A. (Cantab.),
Q.C. (Hon.), Solicitor

Sweet & Maxwell
2002

Published in 2002 by Sweet & Maxwell Limited
of 100 Avenue Road, Swiss Cottage, London
NW3 3PF
(http://www.sweetandmaxwell.co.uk)
Typeset by YHT Ltd
Printed and bound in Great Britain by
Antony Rowe Ltd, Chippenham, Wiltshire

A CIP catalogue record for this book is
available from the British Library

ISBN 0 421 758 902

No natural forests were destroyed
to make this product;
only farmed timber was used and replanted.

Preface

Commonhold is the most radical innovation in English property law since 1925. It adopts the condominium ownership system, which is well known in many other parts of the World, and adapts it to fit in with the established English law rules. It provides a tailor-made solution to the problems associated with the freehold ownership of flats and many other sub-divided properties. Commonhold both overcomes the technical difficulties in enforcing the performance of essential positive obligations and provides a management structure. Many will consider commonhold superior to leasehold, because not only can it be permanent but it can also facilitate eventual redevelopment by laying down terms for winding-up a development.

Commonhold Law, published in loose-leaf form to facilitate updating, will offer a comprehensive account of the law. It will deal with establishing a commonhold, managing it, owning property within it and winding it up. This will be supplemented by precedents of documents, annotated statutory provisions and reprinted statutory instruments.

This *Introduction* gives a bird's eye view of the whole area. Although many of the detailed rules have been left to be laid down by regulations which have not yet been published, the Commonhold and Leasehold Reform Act 2002 already provides the framework. This book is the way in for professionals, developers and property owners who want to understand how commonhold will work and what it offers them.

April 2002   Trevor M. Aldridge.

Contents

Contents

Statutory references

When the text mentions "the Act" it refers to the Commonhold and Leasehold Reform Act 2002.

Statutory citations of a section or schedule, without more, refer to the Act.

Table of Statutes

Non-U.K. Statutes

Australia: New South Wales

PART I

OVERVIEW

Chapter 1

Commonhold in a nutshell

"... a scheme which will combine the security of freehold ownership with the management potential of positive covenants which could be made to apply to successive owners of interdependent property. ... I believe that that the commonhold concept is worthy of, and will receive, wide acceptance.

"Although commonhold has been widely described as a new way to own flats, and of course that is the most likely use for it, it is also available for any development where the occupants owe duties to one another related to their proximity to one another and to the need to manage and maintain common parts of a development. ...

"The standardisation of documentation is one of the most important features of commonhold ..."

— Lord Irvine of Lairg L.C., Lords *Hansard*
January 29, 2001, cols. 455, 456.

> "We cannot legislate for people to love their neighbours but we can provide legislation which makes it easier for people in a block of flats to co-operate and work together."
> — Lord Best, Lords *Hansard* July 5, 2001, col. 900.

OUTLINE

Land ownership

1.1 Commonhold is a new way to own land, specifically designed for a sub-divided property with separate owners of the different parts. The rules are grafted onto the existing property law. Someone who owns this type of property within a commonhold has a freehold estate. Creating a commonhold is voluntary; the existing rules continue to be available for use.

Structure of a commonhold

1.2 A commonhold is a defined area of freehold land, divided into separately owned parcels ("units"). The owners of those parcels of land ("unit-holders") are members of an incorporated association. That "commonhold association" manages the commonhold and owns any communal areas ("common parts"). The unit-holders, therefore, between them own the whole commonhold.

1.3 Any land within the commonhold which is not part of a unit automatically comes within the common parts. That removes the need for any detailed and comprehensive definition of the common parts. Not having to define the common parts is one of the recommendations for the system.

1.4 A "commonhold community statement" must be made to set up a commonhold. This is a document which defines the extent of the commonhold and its constituent parts and regulations governing its use.

1.5 The title to all commonhold land is registered at the Land Registry. The commonhold community statement is also recorded there. Details of the provisions affecting unit-holders are, therefore, centrally and publicly available.

Unlike leasehold developments, a commonhold is governed by a single document. That eliminates difficulties which arise when the separate leases of related properties are inadvertently inconsistent. For ease in operating the scheme, a compulsory form is to be prescribed for commonhold community statements.

A commonhold association is a company limited by guarantee which must be incorporated before land is registered as a commonhold. Its memorandum and articles of association must either be in a prescribed standard form or consistent with that form. The members' maximum contribution on a winding-up is minimal, so they are protected against its liabilities. **1.6**

Commonhold in operation

A commonhold creates, in effect, an area governed by a local set of legal rules, voluntarily accepted by the community which occupies it. **1.7**

The rights and obligations of the unit-holders, the commonhold association and any other occupiers of property within the commonhold are set out in the Act, in statutory regulations and in the commonhold community statement for that particular commonhold. The obligations are made enforceable by statute and continue whoever owns the units. This overcomes the technical difficulties in enforcing obligations against successors in title to those who originally undertook them. **1.8**

The commonhold community statement will regulate the use of units and the common parts and repairs, maintenance and insurance. The commonhold association's expenditure is funded by a service charge levy on unit-holders, in shares laid down by the statement. Reserve funds for specified purposes, to which unit-holders contribute, can also be established. **1.9**

Unit-holders are not always free to lease their units as they wish. Regulations are to lay down restrictions for residential units — where legislative policy is to ensure that long leasehold is not reintroduced within common- **1.10** holds — and the commonhold community statement may limit the letting of other units.

1.11 It is a principle of the commonhold system that each unit should normally be preserved as a whole. So a unit-holder is free to deal with his unit as a whole and he may also lease a part of the unit to the same extent that he may let it as a whole. However, to transfer part of the unit, the unit-holder must, in advance, obtain the commonhold association's consent.

1.12 Detaching part only of a unit and disposing of it separately will mean that its status must be redefined. The detached land has to be made into a new unit, or be made part of another existing one, or even taken out of the commonhold. The cost and trouble involved in the formalities are likely to prove a disincentive to dealing with part only of a unit.

Ending a commonhold

1.13 If all the unit-holders wish to end a commonhold, they may do so by resolving to wind up the commonhold association. If at least 80 per cent of them, but not all of them, vote to do so, there has to be an application to the court so that dissentients have a chance to ask that terms be imposed. The commonhold community statement may lay down the terms to apply on dissolution, but those terms are always subject to variation by the court.

1.14 Creditors of an insolvent commonhold association may apply to the court to wind it up compulsorily. Normal insolvency rules will then apply, except that there is power for the court to make an order which preserves the commonhold as a property unit. It may order the transfer of the old association's functions to a successor association.

USING COMMONHOLD

Residential

1.15 The primary use for commonhold is expected to be for organising the ownership of blocks of flats. There is considerable potential. There were 410,000 households living in privately owned purpose-built blocks of flats in England and Wales at the time of the 1981 census (it seems likely that the number will have increased in the intervening 20 years, but more recent figures do not appear to be available), with a further 147,000 as tenants of housing associations. Commonhold could also be equally useful for converted flats. By contrast, four million flats in France were thought to be owned under the French equivalent of commonhold (*copropriété*) in 1984.

Although flat owning is a widespread form of long-term home ownership, and most are held under long leases, the leasehold system is much criticised in this context. Many people see landlords as predatory and believe that the fact that the property reverts to them at the end of the term is unfair. Whatever the justice of that, freehold ownership of flats will be widely welcomed. Also, most flats, other than those which are just rented on a short-term basis, are bought with the help of a mortgage. Mortgagees would also gain flexibility from the removal of the restrictions imposed by leases granted for limited terms. **1.16**

Finally, the new arrangements offer a technical advantage which renders the recourse to leasehold unnecessary. Commonhold overcomes the law's difficulties in enforcing such obligations as repairing duties and the payment of service charges against successive freehold owners for the time being of the individual flats. It is the virtual impossibility of doing this will now that has all but ruled out individual freehold flats. **1.17**

There are two alternative ways to establish a commonhold, one suited to converting existing leasehold developments and the other for properties which are newly built or just converted. In many cases, the advantages to existing leaseholders of conversion to commonhold may seem marginal when compared with the trouble and expense. But the option becomes important when the current leases are approaching expiry. However, commonhold will be more attractive for flats which have just been built or in a building which has recently been divided. **1.18**

1.19 This was the emphasis which the Government expected when the Bill was introduced into the House of Commons. "We acknowledge that take-up for commonhold will probably be greatest in new-build developments and we anticipate that commonhold will become standard for new-build developments that consist of interdependent units and common parts. However, we expect a unit that is owned freehold to become more desirable and trade at a premium compared with equivalent leasehold properties" — Mr. Michael Wills, Parliamentary Secretary, Lord Chancellor's Department (Commons *Hansard*, January 8, 2002, col. 427).

1.20 In addition to being a way to own flats, commonhold is also very suitable for residential estates where there is an emphasis on associated communal provision, such as recreational and sporting facilities or services for the elderly. The enforcement of positive covenants is still important. But in this case commonhold adds the ready-made structure for management of the common parts which owners will recognise as adding value to their property and will see as central to the way in which they enjoy it.

Commercial

1.21 There are commercial properties the construction of which is physically equivalent to both those types of residential property which are primarily suited to commonhold. There are buildings like blocks of flats — subdivided into units, used as offices, retail shops or workshops, which are separately owned and occupied — and estates of separate buildings sharing common facilities, such as landscaping, parking areas and security. They are just as well suited to commonhold ownership as their residential counterparts.

1.22 Commonhold can also be used to offer long-term owner-ship of part of a larger facility. Parking spaces in a multi-storey car park, or indeed an open-air car park, could be sold in this way. In other countries, properties as small as individual safe deposit boxes have been sold as individual commonhold units.

Mixed use

The units in a commonhold need not all be put to the same   **1.23**
use. Although there may be some complication in the
documentation, units can be designated for different
purposes. Incidental provisions, concerning service
charges, insurance, decoration, etc., can be adapted as
required.

Accordingly, all sorts of developments can be contem-   **1.24**
plated: *e.g.* flats with shops on the street frontage or in a
foyer, offices with flats above, mixed retail and storage
units, a hotel above a multi-storey car park. The
possibilities are almost infinite.

Investment

Commonhold can also offer imaginative investment and   **1.25**
funding opportunities. Consider the possibility of a
proposed hotel development, where each of the bedrooms
is designated as a separate commonhold unit, to be sold for
a capital sum. Although there may be restrictions on
leasing units, unit-holders could enter into management
contracts with the promoters, licensing the use of the
rooms for the hotel business, in return for a share of
profits. The development would thus be largely financed by
investments from the bedroom owners who would effectively have an equity share in the business.

Short term

It will be possible to establish a fixed term commonhold for   **1.26**
a period of, say, 20 years. Although this is undermines the
basis of establishing commonhold as a form of permanent
freehold ownership, a temporary commonhold may be
useful for a property with a short expected life span or
where the proposed use is unlikely to continue for a longer
period.

There is a positive advantage in using commonhold in such   **1.27**
a case, rather than letting the units. Freehold occupiers
would not have the statutory protection which is only
afforded to tenants. So, where the properties are put to

business use, the occupiers could not take advantage of any
right to renew under the Landlord and Tenant Act 1954, Pt
II. Landlords and tenants can agree, under that Act, to
exclude the renewal provisions (1954 Act, s.39(4)) or the
landlord can resist renewal on the ground of contemplated
redevelopment (1954 Act, s.30(1)(f)). But the position will
be more certain if that Act does not apply at all. Similarly,
the statutory provisions protecting residential tenants,
which it is less easy to contract out of, would not apply.

1.28   The way to arrange a short-term commonhold will be to
dispose of the units on the basis that each unit-holder
grants the promoter an option to buy the unit back at the
end of the intended use period. The consideration on the
exercise of the option need be little more than nominal. The
maximum period for which the option could run would be
21 years (Perpetuities and Accumulations Act 1964, s.
9(2)). Provided the option is protected on the land register,
it will be exercisable not only against the original unit-
holder, but also against his successors in title.

1.29   The common parts, owned by the commonhold association, will not have to be covered by any option. When the
promoter exercises all the options covering the units he
becomes entitled to membership of the association, and
indeed he is in sole control of it. At that point he can
resolve to wind up the association voluntarily, to end the
commonhold and to take ownership of the whole property.

VALUATION CONSIDERATIONS

1.30   A commonhold unit is a freehold property which enjoys
certain facilities and involves its owner in defined obligations. That provides a firm basis for valuation. However,
the structure of the commonhold system involves unusual
factors which will have to be taken into consideration when
they apply.

Dividing units

1.31   One of the principles of the commonhold system is that a
unit is generally indivisible. Disposals, other than leases,
must deal with it as a whole. There are certain exceptions,

when prescribed formalities have to be complied with (para. 11.16). They are likely to involve time, trouble and expense. Also, because they will generally require the consent of the commonhold association, the unit-holder may not always be able to do what he proposes.

There is, therefore, a balance to be struck in considering the value to be attached to the prospect of selling off part of the unit, *e.g.* part of a large garden of a house, for building in separate ownership. The prospective profit may have to be discounted for uncertainty. Even if the other members of the commonhold association agree, they may require to be compensated for their consent. Finally, account must be taken of the cost of the formalities themselves. **1.32**

Positive covenants

Enforcing the positive obligations of the owners of separate parts of the commonhold presents no difficulty (para. 11.34). But the general law difficulties inherent in enforcing positive covenants against the successors in title of the original covenantor, remain for obligations undertaken by property owners outside the commonhold. As a commonhold may consist of part only of a building, the valuation implications of this difficulty in the relations between unit-holders and owners of parts outside the commonhold must be taken into account. It could be relevant in relation to repairs, support, protection from the weather, insurance and contributions to the cost of services. It may also affect redevelopment prospects (para. 1.38). **1.33**

Leasing

Although the intention is that owning a commonhold unit should be as nearly as possible equivalent to owning any other freehold property, many units will be subject to restrictions on leasing which may affect their value. The restrictions apply both to a lease of a unit as a whole and to a lease of part of a unit. **1.34**

The unit-holder's power to lease a residential unit will be **1.35** limited by regulations (para. 11.7). In the case of other units, the commonhold community statement may restrict his power. These limits — affecting both the unit being valued and the other units within the commonhold — will often influence valuation, sometimes increasing the value, frequently reducing it.

Common parts

1.36　The facilities which a unit enjoys will necessarily be reflected in its value. The common parts to which the unit-holder has access may afford these facilities, *e.g.* in the form of leisure facilities, parking areas or landscaping. The common parts are vested in the commonhold association which is free to dispose of them; but as a member of the association, the unit-holder will have some say in that. It may be appropriate to enquire whether a disposal requires the sanction of a resolution of the members in general meeting.

1.37　More importantly, if common parts are already subject to a mortgage, their continued enjoyment by the unit-holder is dependent on the solvency of the commonhold association. If the mortgagee were obliged to realise his security, the mortgaged common parts would presumably be sold off and would no longer form part of the commonhold. In these circumstances, unit-holders are likely to lose the benefit of those facilities even if the commonhold survives, under the management of a "phoenix" commonhold association (para. 14.32).

Redevelopment

1.38　A valuer will need to pay particular attention to how practical redevelopment would be. It is normally possible to regard a freehold property as a permanent asset. At the end of a building's economic life, the land will be there and available for use for another building. If the building is destroyed prematurely, insurance proceeds will compensate for the loss, and again redevelopment will be possible. The chance to redevelop is clearly a major factor in underpinning the valuation.

The fact that the freehold of one unit in a commonhold is **1.39**
separate from the freehold of the other parts does not of
itself prejudice redevelopment. On a winding-up all the
property can be vested in a single owner. It can then be
redeveloped as a whole, either in the same way or
differently. But it is only the property within the
commonhold which is available for redevelopment. That
makes it important to consider how far the commonhold
extends.

The destination of the proceeds of the insurance covering **1.40**
the building is also clearly important. Regulations are
going to require that insurance be effected, but it is not
clear whether this will be for the benefit of the commonhold association corporately or for the individual unit-
holders.

Whether redevelopment will physically be possible is an **1.41**
issue. There is no requirement that a commonhold should
include any land below ground level (para. 5.9). So if an
existing building is converted into a commonhold, it need
not include the foundations of it. Clearly, that could make
rebuilding impossible. Even if the current building's
foundations are included, but without any other ground,
building a different type of new building might be
precluded.

LEGISLATIVE BACKGROUND

The passage of the Bill which became the Act was **1.42**
interrupted by the general election called in June 2001.
The Bill was first introduced into the House of Lords in
December 2000 and the clauses relating to commonhold
progressed to the report stage, but it then fell on the
dissolution of Parliament. The Bill was reintroduced very
shortly after Parliament reassembled in June 2001.

The word "commonhold" was probably first coined in a **1.43**
private member's bill introduced in 1980 by Sir Brandon
Rhys Williams M.P. At that time, he applied the term to a
different property ownership concept. That 1980 bill did
not make progress. The term "commonhold" was applied
to the form of property ownership and management which

is dealt with here by the 1987 report *Commonhold — Freehold Flats and Freehold Ownership of other Interdependent Buildings* (Cm.179) (para. 2.28).

Chapter 2

Background

IMPROVING THE LAW

Why commonhold?

Those who favoured the introduction of commonhold saw **2.1** two reasons why it was needed: first, to solve technical defects in the law and secondly, to allow properties which are interdependent to be better managed.

It has to be said, however, that others considered that the **2.2** well-developed leasehold system tackled the problems satisfactorily. Indeed, the authors of one American book considered that the use of leases meant that England already had a condominium system. They reported that its success "has been attributed to the recognized artfulness of English conveyancing practice".

Leases

Leases were originally created to allow two parties, the **2.3** landlord and the tenant, to have separate interests in a single property. However, in the last 50 years it has become common for new leasehold developments of flats to be established in such a way that the landlord of all the flats is a company whose members are the tenants for the time being of those flats. Accordingly, the leaseholders between them own all the interests in the whole development. Collectively, they are the landlord of each leaseholder. To that extent, the arrangement is the equivalent of a commonhold.

2.4 The intrinsic drawback of leases is that they are granted for a limited term. (An indefinite terms is invalid: *Charles Clay & Sons Ltd v. British Railways Board* [1971] Ch. 725 at 731 *per* Russell L.J.). The concept that a property which is leased should revert back to the freeholder at the end of the term is widely misunderstood by the general public. This is particularly so where the tenant or a predecessor has paid for improvements or, under a building lease, has been responsible for the original development. Residential leasehold property in particular frequently seems to be bought without taking the landlord's right of reversion into account. Over the years, many have thought it unfair. The result has been a series of statutes to extend leases, to allow the leaseholder to claim a new lease and to enfranchise, compulsorily buying the freehold reversion.

2.5 Even if the term is lengthy, typically 99 years but it could be longer, there is a seriously inconvenient period as the end of the term approaches. A mortgagee of residential property will normally require the lease of a property which is to be security to have an unexpired term of at least 30 years. Reasonably enough, the mortgagee must not only look at the period over which his advance will be repaid, but must consider the marketability of the property if it becomes necessary to realise the security. Most residential property is only bought with the aid of a mortgage. So any period during which it is impractical to mortgage it, is effectively a period when it is not marketable.

2.6 Of course, where the lessees are, in effect, their own landlords they can agree to renew their leases. Even though this type of development is not uncommon, there is as yet little experience of such co-operative renewals because few such arrangement have continued long enough to make renewal necessary. It seems likely that negotiations could be lengthy, involving all the leaseholders and their mortgagees. The cost incurred would not in reality bring greater benefits than the parties are already enjoying.

Accordingly, an ownership system which is not time limited — which is what freehold ownership in a commonhold offers — is much more satisfactory. **2.7**

The physical life of the building will always limit the period during which it is sensible to continue multiple ownership before redevelopment. That factor will necessarily apply whatever ownership system is employed. **2.8**

Positive covenants

There has been one major technical obstacle in the way of the freehold ownership of separate parts of a building. If the owner of one part of the property undertakes a positive duty — as distinct from entering into a restrictive covenant — for the benefit of another part of it, the burden of that positive covenant does not run with the land of the covenantor. **2.9**

A landowner may undertake important obligations for the benefit of a neighbour or for the common good, like repairing and insuring his property or contributing to a service charge. But as soon as there is a new owner of his property it is impossible to enforce those duties directly. Over the years, ways have been devised to get round the problem — *e.g.* by chains of indemnity covenants, by imposing a liability on those who take a benefit (*Halsall v. Brizell* [1957] Ch. 169) and by using rentcharges — but there is no completely satisfactory solution. **2.10**

This rule that a positive covenant cannot be enforced against a successor in title, which many see as a defect in the law, does not apply to covenants between landlord and tenant. It is largely for this reason that subdivided property has been sold leasehold. But, as has been seen, that results in other drawbacks. Also, even with leases, there are still **2.11** problems about mutual enforceability between the owners of different units.

2.12 Commonhold offers the solution of a regime for the enforcement of property obligations imposed by statute. It applies to both positive and restrictive covenants. That solves the problem within the commonhold.

2.13 The traditional rules continue to apply outside the commonhold and in cases involving relations between those inside the commonhold and those outside it. So, where, *e.g.* the commonhold consists of part only of a building, unit-holders may have problems in enforcing obligations to repair the remainder of the building.

Termination

2.14 Inevitably, there are cases where a property needs to be redeveloped. It may physically have reached the end of its useful life, it may be destroyed or seriously damaged by an accident, changes in the neighbourhood may cease to justify its continued use for its original purpose, or there may be an economic opportunity to be grasped. In all these cases, and maybe others, an easy way to bring the original arrangements to an end, on terms which is fair to all the participants, is highly desirable. Ideally, the details of those arrangements and the circumstances in which they will apply, should be settled in advance. That obviates both argument and delay.

2.15 Existing leasehold developments do not achieve this. Short of premature termination by forfeiture, as a sanction for non-compliance with lease obligations, the leases will continue until a pre-determined date. Only by coincidence will that be an appropriate time to wind up the development. Besides, some of the leaseholders may have statutory rights to extend their leases of which they decide to take advantage (for a house: Leasehold Reform Act 1967, s.2(1); for a flat: Leasehold Reform, Housing and Urban Development Act 1993, s.56(1); for business premises: Landlord and Tenant Act 1954, s.24(1)). There may, therefore, never be a moment when the landlord, even a tenants' co-operative landlord, has all the parts of the property in hand.

Commonhold goes some way towards meeting the need for **2.16** flexible termination arrangements on terms settled in advance. Unit-holders can vote to wind-up the common-hold association voluntarily so as to bring the common-hold to an end. If they are unanimous there should be no difficulty. A voluntary winding-up remains possible if at least 80 per cent of members agree, but they may have to accommodate the objectors.

It is also possible, but will apparently not be compulsory, **2.17** to lay down provisions in advance for the division of assets in a voluntary winding-up. But when the time comes to wind up those provisions may be changed by court order. The simplicity and certainty of the agreement in advance is not therefore guaranteed.

Management

The satisfactory management of leasehold residential **2.18** estates has proved an intractable problem. Over the years, there has been a series of statutes aimed at improving the position of tenants. Among the areas of concern and the Acts which have sought to tackle them have been:

- *repairs* (Leasehold Property (Repairs) Act 1938, restricting the oppressive enforcement of tenants' repairing obligations, originally limited to small houses; Housing Act 1961, imposing a duty on landlords);

- *service charges* (Housing Act 1980, limiting the amount payable; Housing Act 1996, allowing tenants to appoint a surveyor to advise);

- *management* (Landlord and Tenant Act 1987, giving tenants rights to information about insurance and rights to be consulted on the appointment of managing agents; Leasehold Reform, Housing and Urban Development Act 1993, giving tenants the right to a management audit).

These have now been supplemented by provisions in Part II of the Act, which are not the subject of this book.

2.19 Commonhold marks a new departure. The legislation recognises that the unit-holders are freeholders, and that they do not have a derivative or inferior estate. They have full democratic rights to participate in management and the decision taking. There is no separate outside party equivalent to a landlord. Necessarily, however, this means that individual unit-holders do not have statutory rights insulating them from the collective decisions. If, *e.g.* one unit-holder were able successfully to contest the amount payable as a service charge — which is only intended to reimburse the commonhold association for what it has to spend — the solvency of the association would be placed in jeopardy.

2.20 It remains to be seen how far the lack of protection of the position of the individual occupiers will be acceptable, and how far co-operative management will be effective in delivering efficient services. Experience in other jurisdiction suggests that disputes will continue. Provision for an ombudsman to consider complaints offers a way to tackle this.

ORIGIN

International

2.21 The land ownership system which we now know as commonhold is found, although with very different rules, throughout the World. It has many names. In English speaking jurisdictions properties owned in this way are probably most commonly referred to as condominiums, but the developments are also called strata titles, planned unit developments, common interest ownership, sectional titles and unit titles.

2.22 The system was probably first developed in France and Germany, from where it spread across continental Europe. It is believed to have reached the United States from Spain. The first American statute was adopted in Puerto Rico in 1958. In Australia, the New South Wales Strata Titles Act

1961 was seminal. The detailed rules in the various jurisdictions differ widely. There are even areas where condominium ownership is leasehold rather than freehold, *e.g.* the Australian Capital Territory and Hong Kong.

In many federal countries land ownership is a matter regulated by the laws of the constituent states. This considerably increases the number of different systems and the chances of variation between them. **2.23**

England and Wales

In England and Wales the progress towards enacting commonhold legislation was slow, to some interested parties painfully so. Some observers, regarding it primarily as an instrument to right wrongs created by the leasehold system, trace reform efforts back to the Leaseholders (Facilities of Fee Simple) Bill in 1884 (Mr Barry Gardiner M.P., Commons *Hansard,* January 8, 2002, col. 476). **2.24**

In 1965, the *Report of the Committee on Positive Covenants* (Cmnd. 2719) (the Wilberforce Committee) recommended that "a scheme similar to that operating under the New South Wales Strata Titles Act 1961 ... should be made available by statute for voluntary adoption for the regulation of the mutual rights and obligation of owners of units in blocks of flats and other multiple developments". In 1967, the Law Commission *Report on Restrictive Covenants* (Law Com. No. 11) suggested reforms to restrictive obligations which they considered could form a common code with the recommendations of the Wilberforce Committee. **2.25**

Following a consultative working paper published in 1971, the Law Commission published a report *Transfer of Land — The Law of Positive and Restrictive Covenants* (Law Com. No. 127) in 1984 which stated "Our own view is that condominium legislation has very great advantages, and we would certainly not rule out the desirability of such legislation in this country at some future time". **2.26**

In 1985, the *Report of the Committee of Inquiry on the Management of Privately Owned Blocks of Flats,* a **2.27** committee established by the Minister of Housing and Construction, was of the opinion that the strata title system "clearly has many attractions, especially in relation to new development, and many of its features could be incorporated in arrangements for the management of newly developed blocks of flats in England and Wales under the law as it now stands. Furthermore, if all parties consent, similar arrangements could be made for existing blocks".

2.28 In 1987, the report of an inter-departmental working group set up by the chairman of the Law Commission at the Lord Chancellor's request, *Commonhold — Freehold Flats and Freehold Ownership of other Interdependent Buildings* (Cm.179), made detailed suggestions for the rules of a commonhold system. This was followed by draft statutes, published for consultation in 1990, 1996 (Cm.1345) and 2000 (Cm.4843). The Bill which led to the Act was introduced into the House of Lords on December 20, 2000, but had to be reintroduced on June 21, 2001 following the 2001 general election. The Act received the Royal Assent on May 1, 2002.

Chapter 3

Clients' questions answered

Starting a commonhold

Once established, for how long does a commonhold last?   **3.1**

Normally indefinitely. It is a form of freehold ownership.

I have land held on a long lease. Can I develop a commonhold on it?   **3.2**

No. A commonhold can only be developed on freehold land. In a few cases, very long leases — originally granted for at least 300 years, with at least 200 years still left to go, with no rent payable and no provision allowing it to be ended prematurely — can be "enlarged" into a freehold. If that procedure takes place first, a commonhold would be possible on that land.

Why should a commercial developer want to use the commonhold system?   **3.3**

In brief: once the development is completed, commonhold offers a way to dispose of all parts of the property outright; before long, it will be a familiar framework which prospective buyers will recognise and it will not suffer from the risks of careless conveyancing, *e.g.* defective leases; people buying a commonhold unit will not, at any

time in the future, face the loss of value involved in the
difficulty of mortgaging the fag-end of a lease.

3.4   *The owners of flats in an existing block of flats, with the flats
let on separate leases, want to convert it into a commonhold,
must every single owner agree?*

Yes, every owner of any land which will be within the
commonhold must agree. But if it so happens that the
dissenting leaseholder has the flat at the top of the building,
and it is feasible to convert only the lower part of the
building into a commonhold, that is permitted. The rule is
that every part of the property between ground level and
the top of the commonhold (rather than the top of the
building) must be included.

3.5   *Can a single commonhold development comprise both flats
and offices?*

Units within the same commonhold can be put to different
uses. This may complicate the documentation because
different provisions, *e.g.* for service charges and restrictions
on leasing, may be required.

3.6   *Can one unit be both residential and commercial,* e.g. *a shop
and flat over it?*

There can be dual use units. For the purpose of the leasing
restrictions, they may count as residential units, if the non-
residential use is ancillary. In principle, units are considered indivisible and must be dealt with — *e.g.*
transferred and mortgaged — as a whole. So it would be
important to be sure that the two parts of the unit are
always likely to be occupied together. There are formalities
for dividing units, but they involve amending and re-
registering the commonhold community statement.

3.7   *We are mortgagees of land and the owner proposes that it
should become part of a commonhold. He's asked for our
consent. Should we agree?*

All mortgagees must consent before a commonhold can be
registered. Generally, the security is not affected if the land

charged becomes a unit. A mortgage of land incorporated into the common parts of a commonhold is, however, discharged. In one important way, setting up a commonhold will be of grave concern. It automatically ends any lease to which any of the land was subject until then. So, for the mortgage secured on a lease, setting up the commonhold causes the security to vanish. A mortgagee should therefore require a substituted security in exchange for his consent.

What capital does a commonhold association company have **3.8**
to have?

All commonhold associations are companies limited by guarantee. That means that no capital has to be put up at the start. On a winding-up, the maximum that each member can be required to contribute is £1.

Owning a unit

Are there restrictions on the use to which the owner can put a **3.9**
commonhold unit?

The commonhold community statement will say what the unit can be used for. If the only or main specified use is residential, there will be restrictions on how the unit-holder can let it. The statement can also impose general restrictions, such as to do nothing which causes an annoyance to neighbours.

Is a commonhold unit suitable for owning as an investment **3.10**
property?

An investment property is normally let to obtain an income. There are restrictions on letting units, so they may not be suitable for investments. Regulations will restrict letting residential units. The detail is not yet known, but long leases are certainly likely to be forbidden. The commonhold community statement may also limit the possibilities of letting a commercial unit. Each case must be considered separately.

3.11 *Can trustees buy a unit as a flat for one of the trust beneficiaries to occupy?*

Yes, so long as it is within the terms of the trust. Trustees have a general power to buy freehold land and that includes a commonhold unit.

3.12 *As a unit-holder, is there a limit to the service charges I can be called on to pay?*

The unit-holders are together responsible for paying the whole of the commonhold association's expenditure. Each unit-holder's proportion is fixed by the commonhold community statement. There is no ceiling, either as a fixed sum of money or by a rule that the amount must, *e.g.* be "reasonable". Unit-holders are all members of the commonhold association. If they are not content with how the association is managed, their remedy is to vote at association meetings.

3.13 *How does the commonhold association enforce payment of the service charge?*

Service charge arrears are a debt for which the association can sue. There will also be an ombudsman who can rule on disputes. Associations are encouraged to use other forms of alternative dispute resolution, such as arbitration, mediation and conciliation. However, because a commonhold association is not a landlord it cannot forfeit a unit nor can it distrain for arrears.

3.14 *My commonhold unit includes not only my flat but also a garage which I don't use. Can I sell the garage and keep the flat?*

Yes, but it is more complicated than usual. You have to get the consent of the commonhold association, which means that your fellow unit-holders have to agree. The registered documents governing your commonhold have to be amended, so there will be some extra expense.

When selling a unit, can I get back my contributions to a   **3.15**
reserve fund?

The commonhold association may maintain reserve funds for major maintenance items, *e.g.* lift refurbishment. While the commonhold continues, they can only be used for whatever purpose has been specified. But an owner who sells his unit may take the view that his successor benefits from the accumulated contributions. It is quite in order for a buyer to agree to reimburse the seller for what he has paid in.

Who insures a commonhold unit, the unit-holder or the   **3.16**
commonhold association?

The commonhold community statement will impose a duty to insure, and it will specify whose duty it is. So one or the other will have the obligation, there is no invariable rule saying which of them must insure.

As owner of a unit, can I insist that the proceeds of the   **3.17**
insurance pay for repairs and rebuilding if it is damaged by
fire?

The terms of the commonhold community statement will spell out a duty to use the insurance moneys for reinstatement. Obviously, there will be problems if they fall short of the sum needed. Presumably, in such a case, if it was the association which insured, any shortfall will be made up from service charge payments.

If a unit owner fails to comply with his obligations as owner,   **3.18**
what action can the commonhold association take to forfeit
the unit and take it over?

The association has no power of forfeiture. It is not in the position of landlord of the unit. It may have power to enforce performance of a unit-holder's duties, and so may other unit-holders. The commonhold community statement will spell this out.

3.19 *Communal sports facilities are part of the attraction of our commonhold estate. Can one unit-holder prevent the majority selling them off?*

The commonhold association is always free to sell off part of the common parts. It is not yet clear whether it will be permissible to place a restriction on the association requiring all members to agree.

3.20 *Is there a source of day-to-day information for owners of commonhold units?*

The remit of the Leasehold Enfranchisement Advisory Service (LEASE) will include commonhold. Contact them at 70–74 City Road, London EC1Y 2BD, telephone: 020 7490 9580, fax: 020 7253 2043, email: info@lease-advice.org.

Ending a commonhold

3.21 *Can commonhold association members sell out, so that the property can be redeveloped?*

If all unit-holders agree, the association can be wound-up voluntarily. That brings the commonhold to an end. So if an attractive offer is received, the owners acting together have alternative courses they can take. Either, they can end the commonhold and sell the property as a normal freehold. Or, each can sell his unit to the prospective developer and the buyer can wind it up.

3.22 *What recourse do creditors of an insolvent commonhold association have?*

Creditors can apply to the court to wind the association up compulsorily. The association is a company limited by guarantee and each member's personal contribution is limited to £1. In the winding-up all the association's assets — including the balance of any reserve fund, even if maintained for a different limited purpose — will be divided in accordance with insolvency rules.

The unit-holders in a block of commonhold flats may not be responsible for the association's insolvency. Can't the commonhold continue under new management?   **3.23**

There is provision for the court to order that a new commonhold association take over. The presumption is in favour of making a "continuation order". But there will be circumstances in which it is not possible; it is not yet clear what those will be.

What is the nature of the ownership of the land when the commonhold ends?   **3.24**

The land remains freehold. Ending the commonhold simply removes the special commonhold rules and changes the identity of the owners.

PART II

RULES GOVERNING COMMONHOLDS

Chapter 4

General considerations

Nature of commonhold

A commonhold is a defined area of land which is, in effect, **4.1**
collectively owned by a number of people on terms defined
by the registered documentation.

General property ownership rules continue to apply within **4.2**
the commonhold, albeit with some modifications. The
property is freehold. Some is owned by the participants, as
unit-holders, individually; they own some collectively
through the commonhold association.

The mutual relations of the unit-holders, and the way the **4.3**
relations are enforced, are governed by statute. It is,
therefore, immaterial to enquire whether the basis of the
rights and duties is contractual, or to refer to technical
rules concerning the validity of restrictive covenants or the
enforceability of positive covenants against successors in
title. Enforceability is statutory and will be assured by
regulations. They may provide for compensation to be paid
by a defaulter. A provision for compensation must lay

down a way to fix the amount of it and for paying interest on late payments. The court may be given jurisdiction to fix the amount (s.37).

Rules continuing to apply

4.4   Although commonhold is a novel ownership system, it is grafted onto existing basic property law. Those rules continue to apply. Accordingly, amongst other rules, commonhold units are subject to all the following which are not modified:

- A unit can be owned jointly, but four is the maximum number of joint owners of a legal estate (Trustee Act 1925, s.34). The unit can be held in trust, when the number of beneficiaries is unlimited.

- A minor cannot own the legal estate in a unit (Law of Property Act 1925, s.19).

- A contract to sell a unit must be in writing, unless it is sold by public auction (Law of Property (Miscellaneous Provisions) Act 1989, s. 2).

- Stamp duty is charged on the transfer of a unit and on the lease of one (Finance Act 1999, Sched. 13).

- Planning consent is required to develop or change the use of a unit (Town and Country Planning Act 1990, s.57). Additional restrictions, not related to planning legislation, may apply within the commonhold.

- The law of nuisance applies both to safeguard the enjoyment of the unit and to limit the use of it in a way which interferes with the enjoyment of other property, whether that other property is inside or outside the commonhold.

- The resident spouse of the owner of a unit used as a dwelling-house is entitled to matrimonial home rights (Family Law Act 1996, s.30). In certain circumstances, the spouse's rights and obligations are equated to those of a tenant of the unit (s.61).

- A power of attorney can be granted to deal with a unit (Powers of Attorney Act 1971, s.1; Enduring Powers of

Attorney Act 1985, s. 1; Trustee Delegation Act 1999, s.1).

- On the death of an individual owner of a unit, it devolves on his personal representatives (Administration of Estates Act 1925, s.1). If a joint owner dies, his interest in the legal estate accrues to the surviving owners or owner.

- On an owner's bankruptcy, the unit vests in the trustee in bankruptcy (Insolvency Act 1986, s.306).

THE ACT

Commencement

The Act comes into force when the Lord Chancellor makes **4.5** a commencement order by statutory instrument (s.182). No date has been announced. A considerable number of regulations must be made by then, in order to put flesh on the bare bones of the Act, so some delay before implementation is inevitable.

In addition, because two major Acts changing property **4.6** law, which are to an extent interdependent, were passed during the same parliamentary session, there has to be an element of programming. "[T]he Land Registration Act 2002 ... will be implemented ahead of the Commonhold and Leasehold Reform [Act]" — Mr. Michael Wills, Parliamentary Secretary, Lord Chancellor's Department (Commons *Hansard*, March 11, 2002, col. 670).

The Crown

The Act binds the Crown (s.63). **4.7**

In strict historical legal theory, the Crown cannot own a **4.8** freehold, because a freehold estate is held of the Crown as feudal lord. The Crown's interest is properly called an allodium. Accordingly, as commonhold land has to be freehold, it would not be possible for the Crown to establish a commonhold on its land. However, this will have changed by the time that the Act comes into force. The Land Registration Act 2002, s.79(1) gives Her Majesty the power to grant a freehold estate to herself. That will allow the Crown to create commonholds.

Extent

4.9 Commonhold applies throughout England and Wales (s.183). Regulation of this form of land ownership is not a matter which has been delegated to the National Assembly for Wales.

INTERPRETATION

Earlier definitions adopted

4.10 The Act adopts earlier statutory definitions for a number of the terms which it uses. This is a useful way to achieve consistency. This applies to definitions in the following Acts, unless the contrary intention appears: Law of Property Act 1925, Companies Act 1985 and Land Registration Act 2002 (s.69(3)).

Glossary

4.11 As commonhold is a new concept, a number of new terms have been coined. This is a glossary with brief explanations.

Common parts	All those parts of a commonhold which are not designated as commonhold units by the commonhold community statement. The freehold is vested in the commonhold association.
Commonhold	The system of collective and co-operative land ownership introduced by the Act, and by extension one development or estate of commonhold land registered under the Act.
Commonhold assessment	The service charge which a unit-holder must pay to the commonhold association. Strangely, the term is used in the title to section 38, but not in the text of the Act. It is not, therefore, technically a statutory term.

Commonhold association	A company limited by guarantee incorporated under the Companies Act 1985 to manage a commonhold and hold the common parts of it. The members of the company are the unit-holders.
Commonhold community statement	A statement, registered when a commonhold is formed — or as later amended — which defines the extent of the units which form part of the commonhold and specifies the rights and duties of the unit-holders and the commonhold association.
Commonhold land	All the land within a commonhold, specified in the memorandum of association of the commonhold association and for which there is a commonhold community statement. It comprises both the commonhold units and the common parts.
Commonhold unit	A defined part of the commonhold land designated for individual ownership by one unit-holder.
Developer	A person carrying on development business who applies to register commonhold land and who may have special rights to facilitate the development of the commonhold.
Limited use area	A specified part of the common parts which is subject to a restriction as to who may use it or the use to which it may be put.
Registration with unit-holders	An application to the Land Registry to register commonhold land accompanied by a list of the proposed initial unit-holders for each unit, who will immediately be registered as unit-holders.

Registration without unit-holders	An application to the Land Registry to register commonhold land where the applicant will remain registered as proprietor of all the land immediately after registration.
Residential commonhold unit	A commonhold unit of which the use is restricted to residential purposes, or to those and ancillary purposes.
Succession order	A court order to install a new successor commonhold association in place of an insolvent one.
Successor commonhold association	A new commonhold association which takes over the functions of an insolvent association together with ownership of the common parts.
Termination application	An application to the Land Registry that land should cease to be commonhold land.
Termination statement	A statement setting out proposals for the vesting of property and distribution of assets following a voluntary winding-up.
Transitional period	The period between the registration of land as a commonhold, following an application to register without unit-holders, and the first transfer of one or more, but not all, units to someone entitled to be registered as proprietor.
Unit-holder	The freehold owner of a commonhold unit. A person who is entitled to be registered as proprietor of a unit is a unit-holder, even if he has not actually been registered. Statutory provisions frequently apply to joint unit-holders.

Chapter 5

Setting up a commonhold

Freehold land

5.1   It is the freeholder of a defined area of land who decides to create a commonhold on it and to divide it into units. But the owners of all subsidiary interests which already exist in that land, or part of it, must consent. The documentation needed to set up a commonhold is a commonhold community statement, which defines the unit-holders' relations with each other and with the commonhold association, and the memorandum and articles of association of the company which will be the commonhold association.

5.2   It is always technically the freeholder who establishes a commonhold. But there will be cases where the initiative is effectively taken by the owners of long leaseholds in constituent parts of the property, *e.g.* owners of flats who decide that their block should be converted into a commonhold (para. 5.78). They must nevertheless take action through the freeholder.

5.3   In a few cases, a leaseholder can "enlarge" his interest into a freehold by executing a deed poll (Law of Property Act 1925, s.153). This applies to a lease originally granted for at least 300 years, which has an unexpired term of at least 200 years. There are certain other requirements: no currently payable rent of money value, if there originally was one, it must have been released or statute barred; no trust or right of redemption affecting the reversion; no right of re-entry on breach of covenant. An application to register the enlargement of the lease will be necessary before the proprietor applies to register a commonhold.

Outline procedure

5.4   In outline, the procedure to be followed by the freeholders of all the land which is to be included in a commonhold is:

- Agree the extent of the land to be included;

- Obtain the consent of others who have interests in the land;
- Define the extent of the units and the mutual rights and obligations to be undertaken;
- Incorporate a commonhold association as a company limited by guarantee (see Chapter 8);
- Draw up a commonhold community statement which includes the agreed details;
- Register the land as a commonhold at the Land Registry (see Chapter 7).

THE LAND

Extent of the commonhold

The extent of the land included in a commonhold must be defined. The land is specified in the memorandum of association of the commonhold association (s.1(1)(b)) but, in the nature of that type of document, this is not likely to be a comprehensive description. **5.5**

A more precise description is likely to be in the commonhold community statement. The statement must include a plan complying with prescribed requirements (s.11(3)(a)). This plan seems to be intended mainly to define the units, but presumably it will show the extent of the whole development. The conditions which the plan must fulfil are not yet known. It seems likely, however, that where it has to illustrate the subdivision of a building there will have to be drawn to a minimum scale. **5.6**

All commonhold land will be registered. For conveyancing purposes the extent of the commonhold will be defined in the Land Registry's records. The boundaries shown there will not however normally be rigidly precise, because they will be subject to the Land Registry's general boundaries rule (Land Registration Rules 1925, r.278). It would be possible to apply for registration with fixed boundaries (r.276), but that is rare. **5.7**

A commonhold may cover two or more separate parcels of **5.8**

land. It can, therefore, include areas on either side of a
public road. There are restrictions where the different
parcels are parts of one building (para. 5.16). Regulations
may make provision for the case where the separate parcels
are owned by different people (s.57(1), (3), (4)).

Below ground

5.9 The horizontal boundaries of a commonhold, to which it
extends up or down, are fixed by reference to the area
which the commonhold covers at ground level. A
commonhold does not have to include all, or indeed any,
of the land which lies vertically below the area which it
covers at ground level.

5.10 The fact that a commonhold need not comprise all or any
subterranean land is in some ways convenient. It means
that it is not necessary to obtain consents from the owners
of mines and minerals if they are included. Also, underground pipe-lines and railway tunnels can remain outside
the commonhold, even though land lying above them is in
the commonhold.

5.11 There are nevertheless disadvantages in excluding some or
all of the land below ground level from a commonhold. It
could prejudice later redevelopment possibilities. It may,
e.g. not be possible to sink necessary foundations. That
could prejudice the value of units in the commonhold.

5.12 A commonhold can consist exclusively of basement rooms.
This is the one case in which the ground floor of a building
need not be part of the commonhold. Although a basement
only commonhold will be unusual, it is conceivable in the
case, *e.g.* of underground strong rooms occupied as
separate shops. Obviously, arrangements would be needed
for access, but there is no reason why commonhold unit-
holders should not enjoy a right of way for that purpose
over adjoining land.

Above ground

5.13 Similarly, a commonhold does not have to include all the
property above the land which it covers at ground level. In

this case, however, the rules are more prescriptive than for land below ground.

A commonhold need not consist of a whole building. A building can be divided vertically, so that one wing becomes a commonhold but the rest of the building does not. However, whatever the division, the ground floor of the relevant part must always be in the commonhold, unless it is a basement-only commonhold. Upper floors of the building can be included so long as nothing is left out between the ground floor and the top of the commonhold.

5.14

The rule is expressed in terms that an application to register a commonhold must include "all the land between the ground and the raised land [*i.e.* the land above ground level]" (Sched.2, para.1(1)). This means that it can only apply to a case where there is "land" below the raised land. It follows that there is no restriction in a case where there is only air between the ground and a projecting part of an upper storey. So, an oriel window, a balcony or something more substantial, with nothing beneath it, projecting over ground which is not to be part of the commonhold, can be included in an application. Indeed, the commonhold could include a first floor room projecting over a passageway, which is not included, even if the room is in part structurally dependent on the adjoining property which is also outside the commonhold.

5.15

The commonhold does not have to extend to the top of the building. The rule is that if the commonhold consists of any land above ground level, everything between the ground and the top of the commonhold must be included (Sched.1, para.1(1)). The separate rule that a commonhold may consist of parcels of land which are not contiguous does not change this. Land can only be included if everything below it, down to ground level, is in the commonhold. But the freeholder of a flying freehold — consisting, say, of merely the second floor of the building — could include it in a commonhold, if he were to make a joint application with the owner of the property beneath it.

5.16

LAND EXCLUDED

5.17   There are three types of land which cannot be included in a commonhold when an application is made to register it, even though the land is freehold. They are: commonhold land, agricultural land and land held under a contingent title.

5.18   It is to be noted that although Schedule 2 to the Act is headed "Land which may not be commonhold land", the effect of it is clearly only to prohibit an application being made to register these types of land as commonhold land. If there is a valid registration, the fact that some or all of the land later falls into one of the prohibited categories does not prevent the commonhold continuing.

Already commonhold land

5.19   The first exclusion is land which is already in a commonhold (s.2(1)(b)). This means that the only way to transfer land from one commonhold to another, is to exclude it from the first before incorporating it into the second.

5.20   Perhaps more importantly, it is not possible to create a subsidiary commonhold within an existing commonhold. This could have been useful, *e.g.* where a commonhold estate of flats includes open land for later development. The intention could have been that residents in the later development should contribute as unit-holders to the cost of services only to the new block, while at the same time contributing to the maintenance of gardens and drives enjoyed alike by old and new residents. The rules do not, however, allow for that degree of sophistication.

Agricultural land

5.21   The second exclusion is agricultural land (Sched.1, para.2). This is defined to include "land used for agriculture [which includes horticulture, fruit growing, seed growing, dairy farming and livestock breeding and keeping, the use of land as grazing land, meadow land, osier land, market gardens and nursery grounds, and the subsidiary use of land for woodlands] which is so used for the purposes of a trade or business" (Agriculture Act 1947, s.109). The creation of a commonhold is also forbidden on land comprised in a tenancy of an agricultural holding (Agricultural Holdings Act 1986, s.1) or in a farm business tenancy (Agricultural Tenancies Act 1995, s.1). The rules relating to commonholds might be incompatible with those which apply to agricultural tenancies.

It is unclear how far it will be possible to use a commonhold for farm diversification. The system could be useful, *e.g.* for converting a barn into workshop units. Disregarding land which is let, the classification of "agricultural land", which cannot be made into a commonhold, depends on the use to which the land is put. At what point must that assessment be made? The Act is clear in saying that the application to register a commonhold may not be made in relation to land which "is" agricultural land (Sched.2, para.2(a)). The use to which it is proposed to put the land after the commonhold is established cannot therefore be relevant. But it is uncertain whether it would be possible to argue successfully that a redundant barn had no current use — so that its use could not be agricultural — or whether the former agricultural use would be considered as persisting for this purpose. **5.22**

The restriction on agricultural land only applies when the original application is made to register it as commonhold land. It is, therefore, permissible to put land within a commonhold to agricultural use or to let it on a farm business tenancy (unless the rules governing such tenancies are varied to ban the grant of one within a commonhold: para. 11.12). **5.23**

Terminable freeholds

The third category of land which cannot be included in a commonhold is land held under a contingent title, which can in certain circumstances revert to or vest in some other person (Sched.1, para.3). The potential impermanence of this type of freehold title makes it unsuitable for a commonhold. This applies to land affected by reverter or vesting provisions, which take effect when it is no longer **5.24** used for the purpose for which it was conditionally given, under the School Sites Act 1841, the Land Clauses Acts, the Literary and Scientific Institutions Act 1854 and the Places of Worship Sites Act 1873. Regulations can vary the list of Acts to which this prohibition applies.

UNITS

Number

5.25   Every commonhold must be divided into at least two units. There is no maximum number of units.

Extent

5.26   A unit may consist of open land and need not contain any part of a building. It may also consist of two or more areas of land, which need not be contiguous. So, *e.g.* a flat and a parking space or dustbin area could together form a single unit. There is no requirement that there should be any physical delineation of units. So they need not be fenced. Indeed, the units may be parts of a building yet to be built, the extent of which is merely described.

5.27   The commonhold community statement describes the extent of the units. It may describe them in a way which excludes specified fittings and apparatus within the area, *e.g.* providing that mains services running through a unit do not form part of it. The description may also exclude structures which delineate the areas, *e.g.* specifying that the unit is only the space within party or structural walls (s.11).

5.28   It is understood that the prescribed form of commonhold community statement is likely to exclude the roof and structure from units, so that they automatically form part of the common parts.

5.29   It is possible to change the size of a unit by amending the commonhold community statement (para. 12.8). Generally, a unit is to be considered indivisible and is to be dealt with as a whole, even if though it consists of more than one piece of property. A lease can be granted of part of a unit, so long as it complies with the restrictions on letting units (para. 11.10). However, a disposal of part of a unit is only possible with the consent of the commonhold association and it will involve the amendment of the commonhold community statement (para. 11.17).

Factors in delineating units

In cases where property intended to be in single ownership will consist of two physical areas (*e.g.* a flat and a garage), the developer or those responsible for promoting the commonhold will have a choice whether to designate the property a single unit or to make each area into a separate unit. There are a number of factors to be taken into account: dispositions, service charges and voting. **5.30**

If two parts of the property form a single unit, it will not be as easy as it otherwise might to dispose of one without the other. This would be the disposal of part of a unit, which requires the consent of the commonhold association and amendments to the commonhold community statement. In some circumstances, there may be advantages in taking steps to preserve the way in which the development was originally sub-divided, by maintaining the integrity of each complete unit. In other cases, however — such as a development of a block of flats, where some but not all the flats also have a garage, so that it is foreseeable that garages may in due course be swapped between flats — there will be advantages in opting for flexibility from the start. **5.31**

Possible future dispositions also give rise to other considerations. It is not possible to charge part only of a unit (para. 11.17). It may, therefore, be useful to create separate units each of which could be charged on its own, particularly where part is used for residential purposes and part is commercial. **5.32**

Dividing what might otherwise be a single unit would unquestionably take the commercial part outside the definition of a residential unit (into which it would fall if the non-residential purposes were judged to be incidental to the residential purposes (para. 11.5)), so that the restrictions on letting residential units would not apply to **5.33** it. Further, a lease of the non-residential part could be charged, which would not possible if it was only part of a unit.

5.34   The percentages of the commonhold association's service charge expenditure which the commonhold community statement attributes to each unit must total 100 (s.38(2)(a)) (para. 6.22). This appears to preclude the possibility of dividing the expenditure into different classes, so that not every unit-holder need contribute to all of them. It might, *e.g.* seem appropriate that contributions to the repair of the garage forecourt be limited to units which include a garage or that the cost of lift maintenance should only fall on units served by the lift. That type of arrangement seems to be ruled out.

5.35   The alternative — although not making it easy to differentiate accurately between the benefits enjoyed by different units — is to weight the percentages appropriately. This may be made easier if the parts of the unit enjoying different facilities are separated, so that they are different units with their own contribution percentages.

5.36   It is understood that the prescribed form of articles of association for commonhold associations will provide that, on a poll, members shall have one vote for each unit which they own. Whether a particular property constitutes one, or more than one, unit therefore affects the voting power of the unit-holder. However, obviously, if all the units are treated in the same way, parity will be preserved.

OTHER INTERESTS

Consents

5.37   People other than the freeholder may have estates or interests in land which is to be incorporated into a commonhold. Setting up the commonhold may affect their rights. The freeholder must therefore obtain their consent. An application to establish a commonhold is not valid without those consents.

5.38   There are four specified classes of people interested in all or

part of the land whose consent is needed unless a court has
waived the need in a particular case (s.3(1)):

- The registered proprietor of the freehold estate in all or
  part of the land (assuming, presumably, that he is
  himself applying to register);

- The registered proprietor of a lease of all or part of the
  land granted for more than 21 years. All pre-existing
  leases, of whatever length, will be extinguished (para.
  5.49);

- The registered proprietor of a charge over all or part of
  the land. Some pre-existing charges will be extinguished
  (para. 5.44);

- Someone falling within any other class prescribed by
  regulations. Presumably, this will deal with other
  people who have an interest in the land which
  establishing the commonhold will affect.

Examples of people who would have to give consent are: **5.39**
mortgagees, long leaseholders if the lease is registered,
owners of rentcharges, and, probably, those entitled to any
of the following, at least if protected on the register:
easements, options (other than those in leases), matrimonial home rights.

The owner of the freehold or of a registered long lease may   **5.40**
becomes liable to pay compensation to inferior tenants if
he gives consent to the establishment of a commonhold
(para. 5.54). This is because the inferior leases will be
extinguished. A reversioner in that position will, therefore,
be well advised to consult and to come to terms with
inferior tenants before giving consent. The consent is
nevertheless valid even if it is given without consultation,
so the Land Registry will not need to enquire whether
owners of inferior interests have agreed.

Regulations are likely to add significantly to the list of   **5.41**
those who have to consent. The classes set out in the Act
are defined by reference to major interests — freeholds,
leases and charges — protected on the land register. The
rules will, therefore, need to be extended to cover lesser

interests and cases where the land intended for the commonhold has yet to be registered. There are also third party interests which are not protected on the register because they are not capable of registration.

5.42 The form and mechanics of giving consent are to be prescribed by regulations (s.3(2)). They will deal with how long a consent lasts and the effect of giving it or withdrawing it. There will also be rules to govern when consent to one application can apply to another and the possibility that in particular circumstances consent can be deemed to be given. An example of a case in which consent might be deemed given is: a person affected has been served with a number of notices, but without any response (*per* Lord Bach, Parliamentary Secretary, Lord Chancellor's Department, Lords *Hansard,* February 20, 2001, col. CWH13).

5.43 The regulations will also make it possible for a court (the High Court, a county court or a tribunal: s.66) to dispense with consent in specified cases (s.3(2)(f)). A court order can be absolute or conditional and may make other provisions which the court considers appropriate (s.3(3)).

Some charges extinguished

5.44 Some charges over land are extinguished when the land is brought into a commonhold. The test is whether the charge could have been created once the land was in the commonhold. This turns on the rule that it is not possible to charge part only of a commonhold unit (s.22(1)). An existing charge on what becomes part of a unit is therefore extinguished (s.22(3), (4)).

5.45 This only cancels the charge so far as it creates security over part of a commonhold unit. If the charge is secured on a whole unit and part of another, it could and, therefore would, continue in relation to the whole unit. This particular provision does not invalidate a charge so far as it affects land which forms part of the common parts of a commonhold, but a pre-existing charge of common parts is extinguished by other provisions (s.28(3), (4)).

More importantly, any covenant to repay the sum secured   **5.46**
appears to be untouched. It is the charge which is
extinguished; the document, with its contractual provisions, is not avoided. The mortgagee can continue to claim
repayment, even though he has lost his security.

In considering the continuing validity of charges, it is also   **5.47**
necessary to take into account the fact that creating a
commonhold extinguishes pre-existing leases. If a charge is
secured on a leasehold interest and the lease is extinguished, the charge automatically ceases to have effect.

Leases extinguished

The position of tenants of land brought into a common-   **5.48**
hold needs particular consideration. The effect of setting
up a commonhold extinguishes their rights.

Every earlier lease, whether created before the common-   **5.49**
hold is set up or afterwards but before the end of the
transitional period (para. 7.3), is automatically extinguished by the establishment of the commonhold. This
not only applies to registered leases and those noted on the
freehold title, it extends to unregistered leases (ss 7(4),
9(4)). However, it does not apply to statutory tenancies,
which are not true tenancies, but only personal rights of
occupation (Rent (Agriculture) Act 1976, s.4(1); Rent Act
1977, s.2(1)(a); *Keeves v. Dean* [1924] 1 K.B. 685).

The precise moment at which leases are extinguished   **5.50**
depends on the type of registration. Where the commonhold is registered with unit-holders (para. 7.6), it occurs on
registration (s.9(3)(f)). If a new commonhold is being
developed with units to be sold off separately later — a
registration without unit-holders (para. 7.2) — the leases
end as soon as the sale process starts, *i.e.* when someone
other than the applicant is entitled to be registered as
proprietor of one or more, but not all, of the units
(s.7(3)(d)).

Leases have to be extinguished to ensure that unit-holders   **5.51**
receive an unencumbered freehold of their units, and so
that the commonhold association has a similar title to the

common parts. But tenants' rights are seriously curtailed: they face losing their property rights. This is only possible if they consent to the application to create the commonhold. To extinguish a lease without the tenant's consent would probably be contrary to the right to the protection of property in Article 1 of the First Protocol to the European Convention on Human Rights (Human Rights Act 1998, Sched.1), but obtaining the leaseholder's consent ensures that there is no violation of his Convention rights.

5.52   A tenant may require compensation before he consents. There is no restriction on a tenant demanding or receiving payment in exchange for, in effect, surrendering the remainder of his term, and any statutory renewal rights he may have. On the other hand, many tenants may negotiate to receive equivalent rights under the commonhold; indeed in some cases the whole objective will be to substitute freehold ownership of a unit for a lease of the same property.

Short leases

5.53   Tenants and sub-tenants under short leases, granted for 21 years or less, are particularly exposed. They are at risk of losing their interests in the property when a commonhold is established, but their prior consent is not required. For this reason, they have a statutory right to compensation for the loss they suffer.

5.54   The person liable to pay the compensation is the person who consented to the registration of the commonhold who has the most immediately superior title. So, if compensation is due to a head tenant, it is paid by the freeholder landlord. If the holders of more than one superior lease gave consent, because each had been granted for more than 21 years, the most immediate landlord pays (s.10(2)–(4)).

5.55   Clearly, this may result in one person being responsible for compensating several people. The ownership of land might be illustrated:

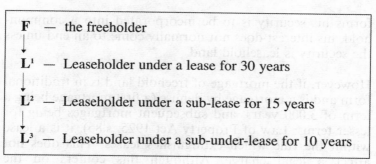

F — the freeholder

L¹ — Leaseholder under a lease for 30 years

L² — Leaseholder under a sub-lease for 15 years

L³ — Leaseholder under a sub-under-lease for 10 years

In this case, both the freeholder and L^1 have to consent. Neither L^2 nor L^3 has the chance to give, or to withhold, consent because their leases were granted for 21 years or less. L^2 and L^3 are therefore entitled to compensation, and L^1 is liable to pay both of them. Even though F must also consent, L^1 pays because he is the more immediate landlord.

Unregistered long leases

Only the "registered proprietors" of leases granted for over 21 years have to consent to the establishment of a commonhold on the land let to them (s.3(1)(b)). So if the lease is not registered, the tenant is not required to consent. There are cases of leases granted before the area in question was subject to compulsory registration of title which have not been substantively registered. The fact that the lease is noted on the superior registered title gives some protection but does not make the tenant the registered proprietor. Nevertheless, the lease is still extinguished once the commonhold is established. For this reason, the tenants under unregistered long leases, and sub-leases, also qualify for compensation for any loss suffered when they are extinguished.   **5.56**

Deciding who is liable to pay compensation is done in the same way as for compensation payable to tenants under short leases (para. 5.54).   **5.57**

Mortgages

Although a mortgagee has to consent if the land which   **5.58** forms his security is to be incorporated into a common-hold, his interest does not normally come to an end unless the security is leasehold land.

5.59 However, if the mortgage of freehold land is in traditional form and is a mortgage by demise (a first mortgage being a term of 3,000 years, and subsequent mortgages being for lesser terms: Law of Property Act 1925, s.85), it is a lease within the rule which extinguishes leases. This does not affect a legal charge. Although this confers on the mortgagee "the same protection, powers and remedies" as if it were a mortgage by demise (1925 Act, s.87(1)), that provision makes it clear that the charge is not a lease term.

Promoters

5.60 The application to set up a commonhold is made by the freeholder of the land. The convenient overall term "promoter", to cover applicants who can apply in different circumstances, is not a statutory term.

Land owner

5.61 The land to be included in a commonhold does not all have to be owned by one person. Several landowners, each owning different parts of an assembled site, can join together to establish it. In the event, the result must be that the freehold owner of all the land applies to register the commonhold (s.2(1)(a)).

5.62 This means that if land is jointly owned, all joint owners must act together. But this applies only to the owners of the legal estate. When the legal estate is vested in trustees, only they are the ones to apply to set up the commonhold. The beneficiaries with equitable interests in the land are not included. However, trustees may well be obliged to consult their beneficiaries before applying, or joining in an application, to register commonhold land (Trusts of Land and Appointment of Trustees Act 1996, s.11).

5.63 There is a small element of doubt whether more than four people can apply to register a commonhold, even though they may all own separate parcels of land which are all

intended to form part of the commonhold. The immediate
effect of a registration without unit-holders (para. 7.2) is
that "the applicant shall continue to be registered as the
proprietor of the freehold estate in the commonhold land"
(s.7(2)(a)). No more than four people can be so registered.
It seems likely, however, that there will be a procedure
(prescribed by regulations, yet to be made) which will allow
more than four property owners to apply for the
registration of commonhold land in the names of no more
than four of their number. Those four would then be the
applicants in whose name the registration would continue.

Existing leasehold developments

An existing leasehold development can be converted into a   **5.64**
commonhold. It will either have a landlord who is
independent of the leaseholders, and who typically can be
obliged to sell the freehold to enfranchise the leaseholders
(Leasehold Reform, Housing and Urban Development Act
1993) (para.5.83), or the landlord will be a company whose
members are the leaseholders. In both cases, the application to set up the commonhold must be made by the
freeholder, but the procedure will differ.

Where the freeholder is an outsider who is selling to the   **5.65**
leaseholders, they will want to complete that transaction
before applying to establish the commonhold. But the
necessary applications to the Land Registry can conveniently be made simultaneously. So, while the purchase of the
freehold is negotiated the commonhold arrangements
should be agreed. On completion of the purchase, the
leaseholders' nominees can then apply both to register the
transfer of the freehold and to set up the commonhold.

In the case of a freehold already owned by a leaseholders'   **5.66**
company, that company can apply to set up the common-
hold in the same way as any other single freeholder.

Developer

The position of a commercial commonhold developer,   **5.67**
whether he develops a new block or estate or refurbishes an
existing one, needs special consideration. At some point

during the disposal programme of the units he will cease to own a majority of them and, therefore, if no special provision is made, will lose control of the commonhold association. Implementing the views of the majority of incoming unit-holders might prejudice him in completing the disposal of the remaining units.

5.68   This problem is familiar in leasehold developments. In that context it can be tackled, where the freehold is to be vested in a company whose members are the leaseholders, either by delaying the transfer of the freehold to the company or by special provisions which give the developer voting control until the final disposal. These solutions are not available for commonhold developments. Instead, the problem is addressed by statutory provisions.

5.69   The commonhold community statement may give the developer rights which allow him to undertake his "development business" and to facilitate it. That business is defined to include doing works on a commonhold, or land to be added to one or removed from it, marketing and advertising the units, varying the extent of the common-hold land and individual units and appointing and removing directors of the commonhold association (s.58(1), Sched.4). The special provisions for this purpose may include requiring the commonhold association or a unit-holder to co-operate, with sanctions for non-compli-ance. If the memorandum and articles of the association permit, they may allow land to be added to the commonhold without the approval of a resolution of the commonhold association (s.58(1)–(5)).

5.70   While the development is still in progress, the developer may transfer his interest in all or part of the property to someone else. From the date of the transfer the developer's successor is then treated as the developer in relation to the property transferred. If the transfer is after the transitional period (para. 7.3), or it is a case where there is no such period, the transfer must be expressed to include develop-ment rights and must comprise more than a single unit (s.59(1)–(3)).

5.71   After the transitional period, or if there is none, a person

can only be treated as the developer if he is currently
freeholder of at least one unit and also is or has been
freeholder of more than one (s.59(4)). Accordingly, once
the developer has disposed of all the units, he is no longer
entitled to his privileged position. Before that, the
developer may send the Land Registry notice surrendering
any of his special rights and he may contract with those
who buy the units to do so in certain circumstances. When
the notice is registered, the Registry informs the commonhold association as soon as possible and the right ceases to
be exercisable (s.58(6)).

Securing development finance

Developers commonly borrow building finance for carry-   **5.72**
ing out a development. They secure it on the estate, on
terms that they repay it from the proceeds of the sale of
each unit when received. There should be no difficulty in
making the same arrangements to carry out a commonhold
development.

This form of commonhold development involves a   **5.73**
registration without unit-holders, where the developer
retains ownership of the units until they are individually
sold and there is a transitional period until the first sale (ss
7, 8). On the initial registration of the commonhold, the
developer remains the registered proprietor of the land.
The charge at that point affects the whole property.

When each unit is sold, it can be released from the charge   **5.74**
and the proceeds of sale paid to the mortgagee in the usual
way.

One variation is necessary from the way in which these   **5.75**
matters are normally arranged. As soon as the first unit is
sold by the developer, the charge will be extinguished so far
as it relates to the common parts, which then vest in the
commonhold association (s.28(3)). Where, as is generally
the case, the common parts are not independently of
commercial value — such as drives and staircases — this
will presumably not be a matter of concern. A mortgagee
which had to realise the security would be able to sell off
the units. Once the sale was completed, the units would

carry with them the rights, including rights over the common parts, detailed in the commonhold community statement.

Developer's withdrawal

5.76   A developer is free to change his mind before the end of the transitional period (para. 7.3) and can decide not to proceed with the development or not to sell it on a commonhold basis. This enables him to respond to changes in the market or in his own circumstances. However, by limiting that right to the transitional period, the position of third parties is protected. Once a unit has been sold, and other owners are involved, the right to withdraw disappears.

5.77   A developer who wishes to withdraw must apply to the Land Registry. The land will then cease to be registered as commonhold land, but the developer will be proprietor of it as a normal freehold. The developer's application must be accompanied by the same consents as were needed to register the commonhold (s.8(4), (5)) (para. 5.38). It seems likely that a relatively high Land Registry fee will be payable by a developer who withdraws; the Registry will wish to deter applications followed by withdrawal, which will involve abortive, unproductive work.

CONVERTING A LEASEHOLD DEVELOPMENT

Preliminary

5.78   Many modern blocks of flats were developed on the basis the flats would be sold on long leases and the freehold reversion would be held by a company whose members would be the leaseholders. Some older blocks were converted to that form of ownership and some estates of houses are owned on a similar basis. This is sometimes seen as freehold ownership by those who are technically leaseholders. (Estate agents' particulars commonly refer to "leasehold with share of freehold".) It is suitable for conversion to commonhold, with its attendant advantages.

5.79   The first step is to check that the property in question satisfies the pre-conditions for establishing a commonhold. If it does, there are three major matters for the participating owners to agree in advance:

- The extent of each unit and the consequent extent of the common parts;
- The percentage of each unit-holder's contribution towards service charges. These may well be defined in the leases, but, on conversion to commonhold, they can be varied if all agree;
- The percentage entitlement of each unit-holder on a winding-up. Agreement on this is not essential, but it can prove useful.

The leaseholders promoting the conversion must then **5.80** ensure that all those whose consent will be required are prepared to give it.

Procedure

A contract, or if more convenient a series of contracts, will **5.81** be required. These are the main matters to cover:

- The prospective unit-holders will promote a commonhold association and apply for the registration of a commonhold, with a commonhold community statement, to define their rights and obligations, in an agreed form;
- The mortgagees of individual leases must give consent. The creation of the commonhold will bring the leases to an end, so the mortgagees' current security will disappear. They will, therefore, have to accept commonhold units as substituted security. The unit-holders will need to execute appropriate new mortgages;
- Sub-tenants under short leases of all or parts of the property must accept that their tenancies will end. Acceptance may be achieved by giving notice, agreeing compensation or accepting that a new term will be substituted. In the last case, the unit-holder in question or the commonhold association must grant the subtenant a new lease or tenancy which he accepts. Any

new lease must comply with any restrictions on leasing commonhold land.

5.82   The new commonhold will then be registered, the appropriate procedure being "registration with unit-holders" (para. 7.6). Each unit-holder will be entitled to be registered proprietor of his unit and the common parts will be vested in the commonhold association. The registration of the mortgages, and if appropriate the new leases or tenancies, will be carried out separately — although, effectively, simultaneously — in the usual way.

Enfranchisement

5.83   There is no formal link between conversion of a leasehold development into a commonhold and the right to enfranchise. But those who wish to convert can usefully enfranchise. Owners of long leasehold flats who do not, collectively, own the freehold of their block but wish to convert it into a commonhold may be able to do so by applying to the landlord to enfranchise collectively. This enables them to nominate a person to buy the freehold.

5.84   In outline, and omitting some detail, the qualifications for the right to enfranchise are:

- The block of flats is self-contained and used wholly or predominantly for residential purposes;

- The tenancies of the flats were granted for terms of over 21 years;

- The initial rent must have been under two-thirds of the letting value or two-thirds of the rateable value;

- The tenants of at least two-thirds of the flats must qualify to enfranchise.

For greater detail, see *Leasehold Law* paras 8.055 *et seq.*

5.85   At first glance, it appears convenient for tenants who are enfranchising with a view to converting their block into a commonhold to nominate the commonhold association as the person to acquire the freehold. This is not, however, possible for two reasons. First, the association is unlikely to have the necessary power. Secondly, once it had completed the purchase, the directors could not give a certificate that it had not traded, which they must do on when the application is made to register the commonhold.

Chapter 6

Commonhold Community Statement

Contents

Purpose

6.1 The commonhold community statement defines the rights and governs the relations of all property owners within a particular commonhold, supplementing the general rules laid down by statute. The areas not included are the matters covered by the memorandum and articles of association of the commonhold association concerning operation of the association. The statement is, therefore, the pivotal document in both setting up a commonhold and in its continuing operation.

6.2 The role which the commonhold community statement plays in establishing the framework of the commonhold makes is comparable to the series of leases in a leasehold development. The fact that it is a single document, so that there is no danger of a mismatch between the contents of separate ones applying to different parts of the property pinpoints one of the advantages of the commonhold system.

Form

A commonhold community statement must be a document **6.3** in a form which will be prescribed (s.31(1)). What the requirements will be are not known, apart from the fact that there will be to be a plan, which must itself comply with prescribed requirements (s.11(3)(a)).

A single statement must apply to the whole commonhold, **6.4** even if it consists of more than one parcel of land (s.57(2)).

Variation

There is a procedure for amending a commonhold **6.5** community statement (para. 12.15). There may also be circumstances in which it is appropriate to rectify it (para. 12.20).

Contents

General

The Act lays down some general rules about the contents **6.6** of a commonhold community statement. In addition, regulations, of which no details are yet available, will provide that specific provisions may, and may not, be included. Those regulations can apply different rules to different circumstances (ss 31(2), 32). So they may, *e.g.* apply differently to units when some are used for residential purposes and others are non-residential units.

The regulations can lay down provisions which a **6.7** commonhold community statement is deemed to include, although it will be possible for them to allow other provisions to be substituted (s.32(3)).

6.8 There are certain statutory restrictions on the contents of a commonhold community statement (s.31(8), (9)):

- They must not be inconsistent with the Act or with any regulations about the contents of statements.

- The memorandum and articles of association of the commonhold association also takes precedence, so the statement's contents must not be inconsistent with it.

- A statement cannot validly provide that an interest in land will be transferred or lost on a specified event. This prohibits, *e.g.* the equivalent of the proviso for forfeiture found in most long leases. Forfeiture itself is impossible because the unit is freehold, but a unit-holder's failure to perform a duty imposed on him by the commonhold community statement cannot result in his being obliged compulsorily to transfer the unit to someone else.

Developers

6.9 In a case where the commonhold is being established by a developer who needs special provision until he has finally disposed of the units (para. 5.67), those arrangements must be made in the commonhold community statement (s.58(2)).

Property layout

6.10 By reference to its plan, the commonhold community statement defines the extent of each of the units (s.11(2), (3)). In many cases this will naturally involve outlining the whole commonhold, but it is not yet clear whether this will be a requirement. It may be that, in the light of difficulties which have from time to time been encountered with plans on a scale so small as to be inadequate, regulations will impose minimum requirements.

> The short point is that the plan [scale 1:2,500] is quite useless for telling one where the boundary is to pass through the house. ... If a house is to be divided and a plan is to form part of the material describing the boundary, it is essential that there should be a large-

scale plan of the house showing the rooms and the walls: *Scarfe v. Adams* [1981] 1 All E.R. 843 at 850—1 *per* O'Connor L.J.

Use

The commonhold community statement must regulate the use of each unit (s.14(1)). This provision is wide enough to allow the statement to require a unit to be put to a particular use. But it seems more likely that it will merely authorise one use, or class of use, and forbid other uses. Obligations requiring that property be actively put to a specific use have proved difficult to enforce: indeed, a lease covenant to keep premises open for retail trade could not be specifically enforced, although damages could be recovered for breach *(Co-operative Insurance Society Ltd v. Argyll Stores (Holdings) Ltd* [1998] A.C. 1). Although the provisions of a commonhold community statement are not contractual obligations, so that enforcement is merely a matter of applying the Act, the inherent practical difficulties would remain.   **6.11**

The permitted use may vary from unit to unit. So, some units might, *e.g.* be confined to residential use while others are designated for use as offices or retail shops. It is not clear what degree of detail in defining a permitted use will be allowed or appropriate. In letting retail premises, leases frequently require or prohibit specific trades for estate management purposes and to maintain overall property values. That degree of detail may not be appropriate in a commonhold, bearing two points in mind. First, there is no single person with an interest in the whole property, as is the case with a landlord. Secondly, the restrictions are being imposed on a freehold and not on a leasehold interest granted for a limited period.   **6.12**

The statement may also restrict the use of a specified part of the common parts, called a "limited use area". The limitation may be on who may use the area or on the use to which it may be put. The statement may apply to more than one such area, and make different regulations for each (s.25). Two illustrations of the ways in which this type of restriction will be useful can be given. First, where some but not all units include garage accommodation, the use of   **6.13** vehicular drives could be reserved for the unit-holders of those units. Secondly, technical areas owned by the commonhold association, such as lift motor rooms and boiler rooms, could be limited to use by authorised staff.

Rights and duties

6.14   The rights and duties of both the commonhold association and of unit-holders (or in the case of joint unit-holders, all of them separately and jointly: s.13(3)) are set out in the commonhold community statement. The statement may impose those duties, which are binding without further formality, and lay down how management decisions will be taken (s.31(1), (3), (7)).

6.15   The statement must also impose other duties in relation to the units, requiring performance by either the unit-holder or the commonhold association. These duties relate to insurance and to repair and maintenance of each unit (s.14(2), (3)). The inclusion of these provisions is expressed to be mandatory, but bearing in mind that a unit need not include any part of a building (s.11(4)), they will not always be appropriate. The provision must presumably be read as applying as and where it can sensibly do so.

Insurance

6.16   The scope of the provisions which a commonhold community statement must make about insurance will not be clear until the regulations have been made. Experience with leases suggests that they could usefully cover: risks to be covered (bearing in mind that cover is not available for some risks and for others is universally subject to an excess), incidental and consequential loss (*e.g.* loss of rent or the cost of accommodation while the property is unusable), the amount of cover (professional fees, the cost of clearance and VAT may need to be added to full rebuilding value) and the type of insurer.

6.17   The provision requiring that a duty to insure is specified includes a duty to use the proceeds of insurance for the purpose of rebuilding or reinstating (s.69(2)(a)). The Fires Prevention (Metropolis) Act 1774, s.83 (which applies throughout the country: *Sinott v. Bowden* [1912] 2 Ch. 414, but probably does not apply to insurance at Lloyd's: *Portavon Cinema Co Ltd v. Price and Century Insurance Co Ltd* [1939] 4 All E.R. 601 at 607—8 *per* Branson J., *obiter*) allows anyone interested in premises damaged by fire to require that insurance money be laid out in reinstatement.

Repair and maintenance

Repair and maintenance are to be construed separately, although there will certainly be some overlap. The meaning of "repair" has been much litigated. The following points should be noted: **6.18**

- It means making good a defect, not merely curing something which has proved unsuitable for its purpose (*Quick v. Taff Ely Borough Council* [1986] Q.B. 809).

- Work goes beyond being a repair if the result is the creation of a materially different building (*Eyre v. McCracken* (2000) 80 P.&C.R. 220).

- The obligation to repair imposes no duty to modernise, although that may be the incidental result (*Lyon v. Greenhow* (1892) 8 T.L.R. 457; *Ravenseft Properties Ltd v. Davstone (Holdings) Ltd* [1980] Q.B. 12).

- Repair includes keeping services working (*Bishop v. Consolidated London Properties Ltd* (1933) 148 L.T. 407 at 410 *per* Du Parcq J.).

- Minimal defects are not covered (*Scales v. Lawrence* (1860) 2 F.&F. 289).

- In the case of a lease, the extent of the obligation depends on the age and nature of the property at the date of the lease (*Lurcott v. Wakely and Wheeler* [1911] 1 K.B. 716). By analogy, this may apply to its age and nature when the commonhold is established.

The Act defines maintaining the property to include decorating it and putting it into sound condition (s.69(2)(b)). Presumably that means complete decoration, both inside and out; "repair" can include a limited amount of necessary decorative work (*Proudfoot v. Hart* (1890) 25   **6.19**

Q.B.D. 42). Leases frequently specify the types of decorative finish to be used. They also usefully contain provisions designed to ensure that buildings in multiple ownership or occupation adopt a uniform exterior style and colour.

6.20 Putting the property "into sound condition" may go beyond what an obligation to repair requires. However, it begs the question: for what purpose is the condition to be sound? As a minimum, the obligation may only mean to make the property wind- and weather-proof. But the duty could extend further if it is to be construed by reference to the permitted use of the unit. The work might then have to meet the standard which those in the market for the particular property would require and it might have to comply with statutory requirements applicable to a property put to that purpose.

Service charges and reserve funds

6.21 Commonhold assessments (service charges) and reserve funds (if any) must be dealt with in the commonhold community statement. As far as assessments are concerned, the statement must require the directors of the common-hold association to estimate the income required to be raised from unit-holders. They have to do this annually and must be authorised to make additional estimates from time to time (s.38(1)(a), (b)). This sum, "the income required to be raised from unit-holders", may not be the total expenditure of the association. If it has other sources of income — *e.g.* rent from letting common parts, insurance claims, the proceeds of a mortgage — they will reduce the amount which unit-holders have to pay.

6.22 The commonhold community statement must require the directors to serve notices on the unit-holders saying what each must pay and when. They must pay percentages specified for their respective units in the statement. Those percentages must total 100, but 0 per cent may be specified for a particular unit (s.38(1)(c)–(e), (2)). As the statement is registered and copies are freely available, the percentage service charge liability attributable to each unit is public information.

The statement may, but need not, require the establishment   **6.23**
of one or more reserve funds for stated purposes. They can
be for the repair and maintenance of common parts or the
repair and maintenance of commonhold units. In each case
— common parts and units — more than one fund may be
established. So, the intention must be that the purposes will
be more specific than repair and maintenance generally.
They might, *e.g.* be for the repair of a lift or for exterior
decoration. If the statement does make provision for
establishing one or more funds, there must be provisions
about contributions (s.39(1)–(3)).

Dispositions

In relation to units which are not residential, *i.e.* not stated   **6.24**
to be required to be used only for residential purposes or
for those and incidental purposes (s.17(5)), the commonhold community statement may contain provisions subject
to which a lease will have effect (s.18). Presumably this
does not allow the statement to impose a complete ban on
such lettings (para. 11.10), as it would be perverse to say
that a lease took effect subject to a provision which meant
it was of no effect. The statement certainly cannot restrict
transfers, mortgages or the creation and transfer of other
interests in other ways (s.20(1), (2)). Nor may it restrict the
commonhold association in transferring any part of the
common parts or creating an interest in them (s.27).

Entitlement on winding-up

The commonhold community statement may make provi-   **6.25**
sion in the event of the winding-up of the commonhold,
but it need not do so. It may require that any termination
statement make arrangements about the rights of unit-
holders of a specified kind or determined in a specified
manner. This means that the shares to which particular
units entitle their owners would be settled in advance.
Commonly, those provisions are likely to specify percentage shares, but more complicated arrangements could
apply, *e.g.* any surplus above a current valuation would be
divided only between the owners of a specific type of unit
(s.47(2), (3)).

6.26   However, when it comes to a winding-up, a court order may disapply the terms laid down in the commonhold community statement. The court has a wide discretion. The provisions may be disapplied generally, in relation to specified matters or for a particular purpose (s.47(4)). There is no guidance about how these powers will be exercised.

Chapter 7

Registration

Contents   *page*

TYPES OF REGISTRATION

All commonhold land is registered at the Land Registry **7.1** and registration specifically as a commonhold is essential. A commonhold only exists when registration is complete (s.1(1)). There are two ways in which registration can come about. Either the registration is "without unit-holders" or it is "with unit-holders".

Registration without unit-holders

A registration without unit-holders is the appropriate **7.2** procedure when the units will not be vested in individual unit-holders immediately after registration. The freeholder applies for registration, and on registration the applicant remains registered as proprietor of the whole of the commonhold land (s.7(2)). Only later, when someone else becomes entitled to one or more, but not all, of the units, the commonhold takes full effect. The commonhold association is then registered as proprietor of the common parts, without any further application, and the provisions of the commonhold community statement come into effect (s.7(3)).

7.3 Necessarily, this means that there will be a "transitional period" between the registration of the land as a commonhold and the disposal of a unit which triggers the full commonhold effect. During this period, the freeholder has the important right to require the registrar to arrange that registration as a commonhold shall cease. Cancelling the commonhold requires the same consents as registering it did in the first place (s.8(1), (4), (5)) (para. 5.38).

7.4 Regulations may modify or suspend the effect of certain provisions during the transitional period. This can apply to statutory provisions, the commonhold community statement and the memorandum and articles of the commonhold association (s.8(2), (3)).

7.5 This procedure, registration without unit-holders, is suitable for a speculative development of a new commonhold, where the developer registers it before building is complete and then sells off units individually. The land is run as a commonhold when the first unit-holder becomes entitled to be registered. The preliminary registration of the commonhold enables the developer to give details to prospective buyers, while preventing the formalities from delaying his disposal of the units. On the other hand, he retains the option to change his mind, abandoning the commonhold concept and dealing with his property in a different way, until he disposes of the first unit.

Registration with unit-holders

7.6 When units are immediately to be vested in individual unit-holders, the appropriate procedure is registration with unit-holders. The only difference in the procedure is that the application must be accompanied by a statement requesting that this applies. It lists the commonhold units and details (to be prescribed) of the initial unit-holder(s) of each (s.9(1), (2)).

The effect of a registration without unit-holders is that the **7.7** commonhold rules come fully into effect on registration (s.9(3)). The procedure suits the case where the current leaseholders of an existing block of flats decide to convert the block into a commonhold. The termination of their existing leases and the coming into effect of their ownership of the new units will be simultaneous.

APPLICATION

Applicant

An application to register a commonhold is made to the **7.8** Land Registry by the registered proprietor of the freehold of the land (s.2). If the land, or some of it, is not then registered, the freeholder may still apply to register a commonhold provided that he has already applied for first registration (Land Registration Act 2002, s.3). In that case, the registrar must be satisfied that the freeholder is entitled to be registered as proprietor (s.2(3)).

Documentation

The application to register the land as a commonhold must **7.9** be accompanied by (s.2(2), Sched.1):

- In relation to the commonhold association, the certificate of incorporation, any altered certificate of incorporation on change of name and the memorandum and articles of association;

- The commonhold community statement;

- Any consents which are required, evidence of any deemed consent and any court order dispensing with consent. If an order is conditional, evidence that the condition has been complied with must be sent;

- A certificate of the directors of the commonhold association that:

  * the memorandum and articles of association comply

with the regulations,

* the commonhold community statement satisfies the statutory requirements,
* the application does not include land which is excluded,
* the association has not traded, and
* it has not incurred any undischarged liability. The costs of incorporation will, therefore, have to have been paid before the association has received any income.

- If required, a request that the commonhold be registered with unit-holders.

7.10 Procedural rules for applying for registration at the Land Registry, and to set the fees payable, are to be made in the same way as land registration rules under the Land Registration Act 2002 procedure, *i.e.* by the Lord Chancellor with the advice and assistance of the Rule Committee (Land Registration Act 2002, s.127; s.65).

7.11 Even after a registration as commonhold land has been completed, the registered proprietor may apply to cancel it during the transitional period of a registration without unit-holders (para. 5.77). In that case the same consents are required as on the registration of a commonhold, but the Registrar has no discretion. The land ceases to be commonhold land and the registered proprietor's title reverts to a normal freehold (s.8(4)).

THE REGISTER

Contents

7.12 A register relating to commonhold land will contain the normal details in the property, proprietorship and charges registers. In addition, there will be details specific to commonholds which the registrar will keep and refer to on the register, both relating to individual units and the common parts (s.5):

(a) prescribed details of the commonhold association, and a copy of its memorandum and articles of association;

(b) prescribed details of the registered freeholder of each unit (except during the transitional period of a registration without unit-holders (para. 7.3));

(c) a copy of the commonhold community statement.

Other documents or information may be added, if it is submitted under statutory provisions.

There is a limitation on the usefulness of the record of the registered proprietor in the proprietorship register. When a unit changes hands, the owner's rights and responsibilities pass from the former unit-holder to the new one as soon as the latter is "entitled to be registered", even before he is actually registered proprietor (s.16). So, the fact that someone is registered as proprietor does not necessarily mean that he is the person who can enforce the rights or be held responsible for the liabilities. **7.13**

Registration in error

When land has been wrongly registered as commonhold land as a result of an error, the register can only be altered by applying to the court. Among the orders which the court may make are that the land cease to be commonhold land and for the alteration of the register (s.6(5)). The order can apply to part only of the land registered as within the commonhold. If it applies to all of it, the commonhold will necessarily come to an end. The court then has the powers that it has on a winding-up (s.55(1), (2)) (para. 14.7). **7.14**

If the court appoints a liquidator in these circumstances, he has the powers and duties of a liquidator appointed by the court after it has made a winding up order (para. 14.8). In addition, however, an order that the land cease to be commonhold land may go further. The liquidator may be required to exercise his functions in a particular way, and his rights and duties may be added to, modified or reduced (s.55(3), (4)). **7.15**

SUMMARY

7.16   In outline, the steps for the freeholder to take to establish and register a commonhold are:

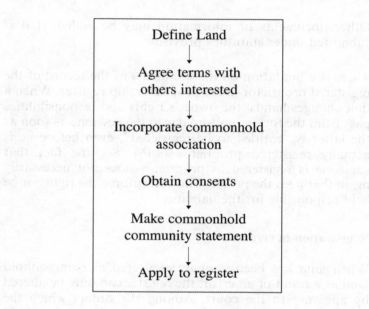

Define Land

↓

Agree terms with
others interested

↓

Incorporate commonhold
association

↓

Obtain consents

↓

Make commonhold
community statement

↓

Apply to register

Chapter 8

Commonhold Association

ESTABLISHMENT

Nature

A commonhold association is incorporated as a private company limited by guarantee (s.34(1); Companies Act 1985, s.1(2)(b)). It is governed generally by the Companies Acts, with specific variations and additional rules derived from the commonhold legislation. **8.1**

Liability of the members of the association is limited. The memorandum must specify £1 as the maximum amount which a member undertakes to contribute on a winding up (s.34(1)(b); Companies Act 1985, s.2(4)). **8.2**

Powers

8.3   The objects of the association will be set out in the memorandum of association. One object will be "to exercise the functions of a commonhold association in relation to specified commonhold land" (s.34(1)(a)). The Act clearly contemplates that other objects may be specified in the prescribed form of memorandum, but it is likely that they will be subsidiary and consequential powers.

8.4   There are two particular activities which a commonhold association will probably be forbidden to undertake. The first is any sort of general trading. The second is ownership of a unit within the commonhold. This follows from the fact that it may not be a member of itself, which it would be entitled to be if it acquired a unit, because a unit-holder is entitled to be registered as a member (Sched.3, paras 7, 9).

Incorporation

8.5   At least two people sign the memorandum of association (Companies Act 1985, s.1(1)). The subscribers remain members of the association during any transitional period (Sched.3, para.6(2)), although after that membership is confined to unit-holders. The statutory declaration of compliance, required before registration of the company (Companies Act 1985, s.12(3)), is treated as extending to compliance with the requirements of the Act (Sched.3, para.17).

8.6   Regulations will provide a model form of memorandum and articles of association of an association. It is not compulsory to adopt that form, but there are two constraints. First, the regulations may include provisions which are compulsory (Sched.3, para.2(3)). Secondly, anything in the memorandum or articles of a particular association which is inconsistent with the regulations is, to that extent, of no effect. Table C, the standard form of articles of association for a company limited by guarantee without a share capital, published in regulations under the

Companies Act, does not apply to a commonhold association (Sched.3, para.4(1); Companies Act 1985, s.8).

In at least one respect the memorandum of an association **8.7** has to relate to the particular land in question. It must state that an object of the company is to exercise the functions of a commonhold association in relation to specified commonhold land (s.34(1)(a)). Indeed, land cannot be commonhold land unless it is specified in that way (s.1(1)(b)).

In some circumstances it will be appropriate to apply to the **8.8** court for rectification of the memorandum and articles of association (para. 12.20).

Name

Regulations are expected to lay down requirements for the **8.9** name of a commonhold association. They are also likely to prevent other companies using names, including a specified word or expression, to prevent confusion or deliberate misinformation (Sched.3, para.16).

This is likely to mean that associations will be obliged to **8.10** call themselves "Commonhold Association" or use the word "commonhold", or the Welsh equivalents. Those are the words which will presumably be reserved for them and forbidden to other companies.

As is the case for every company limited by guarantee — **8.11** other than some in categories which do not include commonhold associations — an association's name must end with the word "limited" or "cyfyngedig" (Companies Act 1985, s.25(1)).

MEMBERSHIP

Members

The unit-holders will be the members of the commonhold **8.12** association. They are entitled to become members when they become unit-holders and, subject to transitional arrangements dealt with below, they are the only people who may be members. The commonhold association may not be a member of itself (Sched.3, paras 7, 9, 10).

8.13 The commonhold association must be incorporated before the application to register the commonhold, so there is necessarily a period after it comes into existence and before there are any unit-holders to be members. Until the land becomes commonhold land, the subscribers to the memorandum are the only members (Sched.3, para.5).

8.14 In the case of a registration without unit-holders, there is a transitional period, between the date the commonhold is registered and when the disposal of the first unit makes the commonhold community statement effective (para. 7.3). During this period the subscribers to the memorandum continue as members and the developer (*i.e.* the applicant for registration of the commonhold: s.58(1) (para. 5.67)) for the time being of all or any part of the land is entitled to be entered on the register of members (Sched.3, para.6).

Members' votes

8.15 Only one person may be registered as a member of the association in respect of each unit. This means that there can only be one vote per unit on a resolution put to the association's members. This remains the case, even if there are wide disparities between the size or value of the units and even if the service charge contributions for each are very different.

8.16 However, although there is only to be one vote per unit, it is understood that the prescribed form of articles of association will allow a person who is unit-holder in respect of more than one unit to cast one vote for each of the units. Accordingly, sub-dividing what might otherwise be a single unit is a way to achieve greater equity in voting power.

8.17 In certain cases, however, the Act requires a resolution to be passed by "at least 75 per cent of those who vote on the resolution" (s.20(4)(b)). This applies where the association is to approve the creation of an interest in a unit or the transfer of part of a unit (paras 11.20, 11.17). To achieve the required majority, one must count the number of voters, *i.e.* association members, rather that the number of votes which they cast.

Joint owners

When units are jointly owned there are rules to decide which of the joint owners is the association member. The joint owners have an initial limited period, to be prescribed, from when they acquire ownership within which they may decide. They can nominate one of their number by giving written notice to the association (Sched. 3, para. 8(1)—(3)). **8.18**

But if the joint unit-holders do not make a choice, the first of their number named on the proprietorship register at the end of that period is entitled to be the member of the association. This, however, does not necessarily achieve the certainty which is no doubt intended. People qualify as joint unit-holders if they are merely entitled to be registered as proprietors (s.13(1)). So, if there has not yet been a registration, there will not be anyone named first on the register, even though there are already joint unit-holders (Sched.3, para.8(4)). **8.19**

In cases of dispute, the joint unit-holders may apply to the court to decide who will be the member (Sched.3, para.8(5)). **8.20**

Which joint unit-holder is to be the association member is not necessarily permanently decided. The joint owners can at any time later nominate another of their number as member, to be substituted for the current member. They may also apply to the court to order a change of the member (Sched.3, para.8(5), (6)). **8.21**

Ceasing to be member

Someone who ceases to be a unit-holder, or joint unit-holder, automatically ceases to be a member of the association, although that does not prejudice any right or liability already acquired or incurred (Sched.3, para.12). He cannot resign membership. This means that membership of the association is co-extensive with ownership of **8.22** the unit, except for a joint unit-holder replaced by a fellow joint proprietor.

MANAGEMENT

Administration

8.23   A commonhold association must have at least one director (Companies Act 1985, s.282(3)) unless the articles of association require more. It must also have a secretary, who may not be the sole director (1985 Act, s.383(1), (2)).

8.24   The commonhold association must have a registered office, of which the address is recorded at Companies House. All notices and communications may be sent there (Companies Act 1985, s.287).

Directors

8.25   The directors of the commonhold association are responsible for its management. In carrying out their duties, they are directed so far as possible to allow or facilitate unit-holders' exercising their rights and enjoying the freehold of their units (s.35(1)). The responsibility extends to the enjoyment by tenants and those with matrimonial home rights under the Family Law Act 1996 (ss 35(4), 61).

8.26   The intention is that it will be open to members to elect directors who are not members of the association, so they need not be resident in the commonhold. A director who is not a member would be entitled to attend and speak at general meetings, but not to vote. The other normal rules about serving as a director apply. So, neither a bankrupt nor someone who is disqualified from being a company director may be a director of a commonhold association. The fact that directors do not have to be members means that there is no danger of the administration of the association being frustrated because all the unit-holders happen to be disqualified from serving as directors.

8.27   Where the commonhold community statement confers special protection on the developer (para. 5.67), he may have the right to appoint and remove directors ("developer's directors"). He will be able to do so during the transitional period (para. 7.3). After that, his right may be restricted and may continue only so long as the developer is the unit-holder of a minimum number of units. A developer's director is not subject to retirement by rotation.

Directors — other than developer's directors — may be paid by the association. Any remuneration must be voted by a general meeting. Presumably, developer's directors may be paid by the developer. All directors may be paid expenses by the association. **8.28**

A director who was a unit-holder when appointed ceases to be a director when he is no longer a member of the association, *i.e.* when he ceases to be a unit-holder. His office is automatically vacated. **8.29**

Directors who have a material interest in contracts to be entered into by the association must declare the nature and extent of those interests. A director may vote on matters in which he has a direct or indirect interest. Provided directors do declare their interests, they may be a party to such a transaction, may be interested in a corporate body with which the association deals and are not liable to account for benefits received. A developer's director is to be expressly authorised to give the developer information he receives because he is a director. That disclosure will not be a breach of duty as a director. **8.30**

No contractual provision can exempt a director from liability for negligence, default, breach of duty or breach of trust (Companies Act 1985, s.310(1)). But if he has acted honestly and reasonably the court may relieve him from liability, in whole or part, if in all the circumstances he ought fairly to be excused (1985 Act, s.727(1)). A director acts reasonably for this purpose if he acts "in the way in which a man of affairs dealing with his own affairs with reasonable care and circumspection could reasonably be expected to act" (*Re Duomatic Ltd* [1969] Ch. 365 at 377 *per* Buckley J.). **8.31**

General meetings

8.32 An association will have to have at least two general meetings of members each year, *i.e.* at least one extraordinary general meeting in addition to the annual general meeting. Notice of meetings will have to be given to all members, but in addition a copy of the notice convening the meeting, and of the documents which accompanied it, will have to be posted in a conspicuous place in or on the common parts.

8.33 A quorum of members will be prescribed, but the level of this has not yet been decided. The attendance of a proxy appointed by a member will count towards the quorum.

Voting

8.34 A number of the Act's provisions depend on the commonhold association passing a resolution. The requirement is only satisfied if every member is given the opportunity to vote, in accordance with a relevant provision of the memorandum and articles of association or the commonhold community statement (s.36(1), (2)). Pending publication of the prescribed form of articles of association, it is not clear how the absence abroad, illness or death of a member will impact on this.

8.35 Votes must be cast in accordance with a provision in the memorandum and articles of the association or in the commonhold community statement. That will provide for voting by post, by proxy or in some other way (s.36(3)).

8.36 Some resolutions require unanimity, but confusingly this term does not bear it normal meaning. It does not mean, as strictly it should, that everyone eligible to vote has voted in favour. Rather it requires that all those who cast a vote voted in favour (*i.e. nem. con.*) (s.36(4)). There is no procedure for applying to the court to override the vote of a member who unreasonably opposes a resolution, so there is the danger of overwhelming majority of members being held to ransom by a minority.

Records and returns

A commonhold association must generally keep the **8.37** records that are required of other companies limited by guarantee. So, it is required to maintain registers of members, of directors and secretaries and of charges, minutes of meetings and accounting records (Companies Act 1985, ss 221, 288, 352, 382, 407). It must also make annual returns and notify the companies' registrar of the address of its current registered office and particulars of its directors and secretaries and of any charges it creates (1985 Act, ss 287, 288, 363, 399).

Members of the association are to have the right to inspect **8.38** any of the association's accounting records, books or documents. This is in addition to statutory rights and rights given by the commonhold community statement. Presumably, this will serve both to enhance democratic control of the association and to provide a way to satisfy queries raised when a unit is to change hands.

There is power to make regulations relating specifically to **8.39** the registers of members of commonhold associations. They would be aimed at imposing time limits on the association performing its duty to register and cancel the registration of members. Contravention could incur to a fine (Sched.3, para.14).

Chapter 9

Managing a commonhold

9.1 The management of the commonhold in accordance with the terms of the commonhold community statement is the responsibility of the commonhold association. This is the effect of the object which the association is required to have in its memorandum of association is "to exercise the functions of a commonhold association in relation to specified commonhold land" (s.34(1)(a)).

UNITS

Use and services

9.2 The permitted use of each unit must be stated by the commonhold community statement (s.14(1)). The same use does not have to be specified for every unit. The regulation of the use of individual units might be more detailed (para. 6.11), although this would generally be inconvenient and seems unlikely.

The statement imposes duties in relation to units. Some are compulsory. They must relate to insurance (and using the proceeds to rebuild or reinstate: s.69(2)(a)), repair and maintenance (including decorating and putting them into sound condition: s.69(2)(b)). Presumably they may go further. The mandatory duties may be for compliance either by the unit-holder (or in the case of joint unit-holders, all of them together: s.13(2)) or by the commonhold association (s.14(2), (3)). **9.3**

This flexibility means that there will not be a single arrangement covering all commonholds. Services may or may not be provided centrally and presumably separate arrangements could apply to different services, so that each unit-holder was responsible for repairing his own unit, but all units might be insured by the association. Comparisons may be further complicated because in some cases walls and fixtures may be excluded from units. **9.4**

Enforcement

Where the obligations are placed on the unit-holders, or the occupiers of the units, the directors of the commonhold association are required to use enforcement powers to ensure that unit-holders and their tenants comply with the commonhold community statement and the Act (s.35(1), (2), (4)). But in doing so, they are directed to have regard to two mitigating considerations. **9.5**

First, the directors must consider establishing and maintaining harmonious relationships between all unit-holders and tenants. If they consider that inaction is in the best interests of those relationships, they need not take action provided they also consider that that will not cause significant loss or significant disadvantage to unit-holders other than the defaulter (s.35(3)(a)). Directors who decide to do nothing will be well advised to minute the decision and the reasons for it. **9.6**

9.7   Understandable though the sentiment behind the provision
to take account of harmonious relations is, it is likely to
cause directors of commonhold associations a great deal of
trouble. Disputes between neighbouring unit-holders will
generally turn on the fact that inaction favours one party at
the expense of the other. Declining to enforce payment of
service charge arrears can only cast greater burdens on
other unit-holders. The question is then whether the loss to
other unit-holders is "significant". This must be judged in
relation to the loss to any one individual unit-holder; it
does not refer to the total loss faced by the whole body of
unit-holders.

9.8   In exercising their discretion, the directors may exacerbate
the antagonism. The difficulties are only likely to be made
worse if the directors themselves are residents of the
commonhold. They would need to be punctilious about
declaring their interests.

9.9   The second caveat applied to the exercise of the directors'
enforcement powers requires them to have regard to the
desirability of using arbitration, mediation, conciliation or
the services of the ombudsman (para. 9.12) rather than
legal proceedings, wherever possible (s.35(3)(b)). Presumably, comparative costs and the time likely to be taken will
be relevant factors here, particularly in dealing with service
charge arrears.

9.10   Because of the constraints on recovering service charge
arrears from a unit-holder's successor in title (para. 10.34),
speedy proceedings against a unit-holder who is in debt to
the association may be important.

9.11   The limitation period for bringing an action to enforce a
commonhold duty, whoever brings it, is six years from the
date the cause of action arose (Limitation Act 1980, s.19A;
Sched.5, para.4).

OMBUDSMAN

9.12   It is the intention to set up at least one ombudsman scheme
approved by the Lord Chancellor and there are powers in
the Act to do so (s.42). Associations would be members of

a scheme and regulations could require them to be members.

The ombudsman will be concerned with disputes between 9.13 the association and a unit-holder, which includes the tenant of a unit (s.42(5)). The scheme will not cover disputes between unit-holders, nor those between a unit-holder and his tenant.

Disputes can be referred to the ombudsman by a unit- 9.14 holder, a tenant of a unit or the association, and the ombudsman has a duty to investigate and determine the dispute. The association has a duty to co-operate with the ombudsman and comply with his decision (including any requirement to pay money). No equivalent duty is placed on the unit-holder or tenant, although the Act allows an approved scheme to contain other provisions.

If the association fails to comply with regulations relating 9.15 to an ombudsman scheme, a unit-holder or a tenant may apply to the High Court for an order which requires the directors to ensure that it does (s.42(3)).

COMMON PARTS

Ownership

The freehold in the common parts is vested in the 9.16 commonhold association (ss 7(3)(a), 9(3)(a)).

Any charge which exists over the common parts before 9.17 they are transferred to the association, whether on the original establishment of the commonhold or on a later extension, is extinguished (s.28(3), (4)).

Extent

The "common parts" are every part of the commonhold 9.18 which the commonhold community statement does not designate as a unit. It is not, therefore, necessary, or indeed possible, to define what constitutes the common parts. This usefully avoids the need for any lengthy formulation which attempts a comprehensive definition. To bring part of the property within the common parts, it can either simply not be mentioned when other parts are included within the units, or it can be expressly excluded from a unit, *e.g.* by defining a unit as excluding structural walls or mains supply and drainage pipes.

9.19   It is not the nature of the property or of its use which determines whether it is included in the common parts. So one flat in a block set aside for occupation by a caretaker employed by the commonhold association and not designated as a unit would be part of the common parts. The fact that it was physically indistinguishable from the other units would not be relevant.

Management

9.20   The management of the common parts is the responsibility of the commonhold association, as the owner of them. The intention is that the structure of the association, effectively giving one vote per unit, will give democratic accountability to the management although the immediate control will be in the hands of the directors. It is open to the association to employ a staff or independent agents to provide services.

9.21   The use, insurance (including using the proceeds for rebuilding or reinstatement: section 69(2)(a)) and repair and maintenance (including decoration and putting them into sound condition: section 69(2)(b)) of common parts must be dealt with by the commonhold community statement (s.26). The association's directors may have a duty to maintain a reserve fund for the repair and maintenance costs.

9.22   The common parts are not necessarily available for use by all members of the commonhold association. The commonhold community statement may specify "limited use areas" for use only by a certain class of people and for a certain purpose (s.25). A caretaker's flat is one example. Others might be boiler rooms and lift motor rooms only for use by engineering staff and a garage forecourt only for use only by unit-holders whose unit includes a garage.

Mortgaging

The commonhold association can create a legal charge over all or of some the common parts, but only if the members approve (s.29). A resolution approving it must be passed unanimously (which means *nem. con.*: s.36(4)) before the mortgage is created. The likely reason for raising money on mortgage would be to finance substantial repair or improvement costs. If the association had not accumulated a sufficient reserve fund, that would be a way to spread the expense over a period of time. **9.23**

The members must give prior approval because if the mortgagee later takes action to realise its security, that might materially prejudice the value of the units, *e.g.* by depriving them of significant common facilities. However, this is unlikely to be a situation which will frequently arise, because the commercial value of common parts assessed independently will often be limited and not suitable as security for a mortgage. **9.24**

Disposal

The commonhold association may dispose of the freehold of any of the common parts or create an interest (other than a charge) over them. The commonhold community statement cannot prevent or restrict this (s.27). Necessarily, common parts which are sold to an outsider (as distinct from being added to one of the units) will cease to be commonhold land. **9.25**

A disposal may be significant and, if, *e.g.* it were the sale of a flat formerly used by a caretaker, could impact on the services afforded to unit-holders. For this reason, it is highly desirable that the implications should be fully considered by the unit-holders before the sale takes place. It is assumed that a requirement that members must vote in advance to approve a disposal would not be considered a forbidden restriction on the association's ability to dispose. **9.26**

The fact that the association can create an interest in the common parts means that it can grant a lease of them. Specified areas of the common parts, *e.g.* part of a car **9.27** park, could, therefore, be let to a unit-holder. The effect would be to give one unit-holder exclusive use of that part of the common parts, albeit on paying a rent. Whether or not that is permissible depends on the provisions of the commonhold community statement

9.28 Exceptionally, to sell off a particular piece of the common parts can mean that the remaining property appears no longer to qualify as a commonhold. If, *e.g.* the commonhold association seeks to sell a flat which was formerly been occupied by a caretaker and that flat was on the first floor, the building without that flat may not comply with the rule that a commonhold must include all the property between the ground and the top of the commonhold (para. 5.16).

9.29 However, that provision does not in fact require that a commonhold permanently include all the land between ground level and the top of the commonhold. Rather, the statutory rule is that no application may be made to register a new commonhold if the property does not comply (Sched.2, para.1(1)). All the same, before the association approves the sale, directors and members should consider its impact on, and significance for, redevelopment prospects.

SERVICE CHARGES

Collection

9.30 The commonhold community statement must make provision for unit-holders to pay a charge to cover the commonhold association's expenses. (This is referred to in a sub-heading in the Act as a "commonhold assessment", but that term is not used in the text of the Act). The total sum the association needs to raise is to be estimated annually, but the directors have power to make additional estimates at any time (s.38(1)(a), (b)).

9.31 The percentage payable for each unit is specified by the commonhold community statement. Those percentages must total 100, so that the association makes neither a profit nor a shortfall, but a unit may be exempted by having a contribution of 0 per cent. The directors must serve notices on each unit-holder (or in the case of joint unit-holders, all of them together: s.13(2)) specifying what has to be paid (s.38(1)(c)—(e), (2)).

Arrears

Arrears of service charge payments are a serious matter for a commonhold association. As the payments are calculated to cover 100 per cent of the association's expenditure, and no more, failure to collect any payments will create a deficit. Any debts which are irrecoverable will inevitably have to be added to future charges levied on those who pay. So if one unit-holder does not pay, his dues fall on the shoulders of the others. **9.32**

When a unit changes hands, the successor unit-holder is not liable for any arrears left unpaid by his predecessor. This presents the association with enforcement problems, because pursuing the former unit-holder may be unprofitable or impractical if he is insolvent or his whereabouts is unknown. **9.33**

This contrasts with the case of leasehold property where a service charge has accrued due under a lease. The effect of the landlord's right to forfeit is effectively to charge the outstanding sum on the property. The current leaseholder must pay if he is to avoid forfeiture. However, no right to forfeit applies to commonhold. Similarly, because there is no landlord and tenant relationship between the association and the unit-holders, distress cannot be used where it might be to recover service charges payable for commercial units. **9.34**

The only way in which arrears can be charged on the unit, unless it is done voluntarily, is by obtaining and registering a charging order. **9.35**

But there are two reasons why a charging order may not be effective. First, a charging order will rank in priority after existing charges. So, the claims of mortgagees will have to be satisfied first, and if a prior mortgagee realises its security the charging order will be overridden. Secondly, **9.36** the unit must still be owned by the defaulting unit-holder when the charging order is made. No security can be created if, before the date of the order, the unit has already changed hands and the arrears are the liability of a former owner.

Reserve funds

9.37   The regulations prescribing the contents of commonhold community statements may require the directors of the commonhold association to establish one or more funds to finance the repair and maintenance of common parts or of the units (s.39(1)). It is likely that this power will be used to require the establishment of funds in residential developments but not where units are used for commercial purposes.

9.38   Where a fund is established, the directors of the association must set a levy from time to time for unit-holders to pay into it. They must give notice to each unit-holder (or in the case of joint unit-holders, to all of them together: section 13(2)) saying what to pay and when payment is due. Again, percentages totalling 100 are to be fixed for units, although a unit may have a percentage of 0 (s. 39(2),(3)). There is no requirement that the statement should specify the same percentages for the service charge and the reserve fund levy.

9.39   The reserve fund assets are ring-fenced for use on the specified purposes. They cannot be used to pay a debt enforced by a judgment or under the Charging Orders Act 1979, unless it was incurred for those purposes (s.39(4), (5)). That restriction ceases to apply, however, when the commonhold ceases, whether as a result of a winding-up order, a voluntary winding-up resolution or a court order releasing land from the commonhold because it was wrongly registered or a document is rectified (s.56). The balance of the reserve fund is then available to satisfy the general debts of the association.

NEIGHBOURS

9.40   Relations within the commonhold are regulated by the

commonhold community statement and the memorandum
and articles of association of the commonhold association.
These documents do not, however, bind landowners
outside the commonhold. Subject to express statutory
provisions, the normal rules therefore apply, with the
possible complicating factor that each unit-holder is the
freeholder of his unit, so there may have to be negotiations
with more people.

A unit-holder has power create an interest over part only of   **9.41**
a commonhold unit, but only with the prior consent of the
commonhold association or with the association joining in
the grant (para. 11.20). An instrument which purports to
create an interest but which does not comply with that
requirement is void (s.20(1), (3), (5)). This applies to the
creation of most easements, *e.g.* to the grant of a right of
drainage or passage of water through a pipe in a unit. A
commonhold association may create an interest in part
only of the common parts (s.27(1)).

The intention may well be that a pipe or wire, for which an   **9.42**
easement is to be granted, will pass through or be attached
to the exterior wall as well as other parts of a unit. Bearing
in mind that the structure may be included in the common
parts, particularly in a block of flats (para. 5.28), the
practical procedure may be for the easement to be granted
jointly by the unit-holder and the commonhold association.

The freeholders of land within the commonhold, *i.e.* the   **9.43**
unit-holders in respect of the units and the commonhold
association in relation to the common parts, will be
"owners" for the purposes of the Party Walls etc., Act
1996. A neighbour who wants to exercise statutory rights in
relation to party walls will have to give notice to all the
affected owners.

Chapter 10

Acquiring a unit

Freedom to acquire and dispose

10.1 A commonhold unit can be freely disposed of and acquired as a whole. The commonhold community statement may not contain anything which would prevent or restrict this. Accordingly, a unit may be sold, given away and transferred by operation of law on death or bankruptcy. Dispositions may be subject to reservations or other terms (s.15(1), (2)).

10.2 It is a principle of the commonhold system that a unit should only generally be dealt with as an integral whole (with a necessary exception in the case of compulsory purchase: para. 10.28). Nevertheless, a dealing with part only of a unit is possible with the commonhold association's consent (para. 11.17).

The rule preventing a commonhold community statement **10.3**
from restricting the transfer of a unit (s.15(2)) appears to
rule out the possibility of imposing qualifications for those
who would be entitled to acquire a unit. That means that it
would not be possible to stipulate that a person acquiring
must be over a certain age. Commonhold would, therefore,
be unsuitable for creating housing specifically designed for
the elderly. (The law has separately recognised the need for
special treatment for such developments. Shared ownership
leases granted by registered social landlords which have to
be held by tenants aged at least 55 do not carry the right to
individual enfranchisement or an extended lease: Housing
Association Shared Ownership Leases (Exclusion from
Leasehold Reform Act 1967 and Rent Act 1977) Regulations 1987.

OWNERSHIP

Joint ownership

Joint buyers may together buy a commonhold unit. The **10.4**
maximum number of joint owners is four. This is because
no more than four people can jointly own the legal estate in
land (Trustee Act 1925, s.34). If a greater number of people
want joint ownership, they must vest the legal estate in no
more than four of their number and create a trust of land,
under which all can have beneficial interests in equity.

If more than one person is registered or entitled to be **10.5**
registered as proprietor of the unit, they are joint unit-
holders (s.13(1)). However, only one of them may be a
member of the commonhold association (para. 8.18).

A transfer to joint buyers should declare the proportionate **10.6**
shares in the unit which each will take. An express
statement is conclusive (*Brykaert v. Jones* (1981) 125 S.J.
323). If they take in unequal shares, or even with an express
declaration of equal shares (*Re Davies* [1950] 1 All E.R.
120), there will be a tenancy in common. It has been
suggested that it is negligent of a solicitor to draw a
transfer which does not make clear the capacity in which
the buyers are taking the property (*Walker v. Hall* [1984] 5
F.L.R. 126).

10.7 If joint buyers do not declare the shares in which they take the property, no doubt there will be an application of

> ... the age-old principle that if two (or more) persons purchase property in their joint names and there has been no declaration of trusts on which they are to hold the property, they will, as a matter of law in the absence of evidence to the contrary, hold the property on a resulting trust for the persons who provided the purchase money in the proportions in which they provided it: *Springette v. Defoe* (1992) 65 P.&C.R. 1 at 4 *per* Dillon L.J.

Multiple ownership

10.8 There will be cases in which the owner of a unit decides to buy another unit in the same commonhold, maybe two flats in the same block. It would be possible to amend the terms of the commonhold community statement to amalgamate the two units into one (para. 12.15). When the intention is to occupy and treat both units as if they were one, this may seem the appropriate course.

10.9 However, even putting aside the trouble and expense of the procedure to vary the documentation, there may be reasons why it may not be the best course. If there is the possibility that the owner may in the future want to deal with the two units separately, this will be easier and cheaper if they are kept distinct. Otherwise, the unit-holder needs the consent of the commonhold association and the commonhold community statement will have to be amended again (para. 11.17).

10.10 Also, the owner of two separate units would, on a poll, have two votes on resolutions of the commonhold association. Further, if the owner of two separate units vests one of them in a nominee, he could control two votes on a show of hands. Amalgamating the units would sacrifice that advantage.

PROCEDURE

10.11 The basic procedure for buying and selling a commonhold unit is the same as for other real property. The seller can choose to sell by private treaty, by public auction or may adopt a variant such as sale by tender. The buyer will wish to make preliminary investigations in the usual way. These should extend specifically to the working of the commonhold. The acquisition will be completed by a transfer followed by registration at the Land Registry (or, in due course, as is appropriate under a new electronic procedure).

When a unit has changed hands, whether as a result of a **10.12** sale or for some other reason, there is an additional duty which does not affect other freeholds. The new unit-holder (or in the case of joint unit-holders, all of them together: s.13(2)) must notify the commonhold association of the transfer. Regulations can prescribe how and in what form this is to be done, during what period and lay down sanctions for failure (s.15(3), (4)). This is the equivalent of giving notice of an assignment of a lease to the landlord.

Ownership documents

The unit-holder of a commonhold unit has the following **10.13** documentation:

- Land certificate (or charge certificate held by his mortgagee) relating to his unit;

- Copy of the commonhold community statement. The statement is filed at the Land Registry;

- Copy of the memorandum and articles of association of the commonhold association. This is filed at Companies House with a copy filed at the Land Registry. There is no share certificate because, as a company limited by guarantee, the association has no share capital;

- Copy of the entries on the register relating to the common parts. This is not essential, but may prove useful.

The obvious difference between this and a leasehold **10.14** property is that the owner of a commonhold unit does not have a document exclusively devoted to the ownership of his property, in the way that his lease would be. His rights and duties in relation to his property and the rest of the commonhold are regulated by the commonhold community statement.

10.15   A prospective purchaser will need to understand what his position will be. The task of explaining it will be less onerous than in the case of leasehold property, because the prescribed standard forms of commonhold community statement and memorandum and articles will become familiar to professional advisers. Further, the differences from one development to another will be minimised, so that someone who has owned a commonhold unit before will know what to expect when buying another.

10.16   It is important that the prospective buyer ensures that he has an up to date copy of the commonhold community statement. The statement can be amended, and when it is, an amended copy must be registered and is then referred to on the register (s.33(3), (4)). Regulations have not yet been made to lay down the way in which the statement will be referred to on the register. It is to be hoped that the date of the statement, or the last amendment, will be included. This would enable a prospective buyer to check easily whether he has a copy of the correct version, and would also allow him to search the register and obtain priority.

Preliminary investigations

10.17   Someone interested in acquiring a commonhold unit should make all the usual searches, enquiries and investigations. These will cover such matters as the facilities available, the physical state of the property, planning and building regulation questions. A copy of the commonhold community statement should be supplied to the prospective unit-holder. From this, he will need to ascertain whether there are matters specific to the property which are of concern — *e.g.* restrictions on leasing, on the use of specified areas of the common parts and on the use of the unit — and he will raise any necessary enquiries about the application and observance of those provisions.

10.18   In addition, there will be questions specific to the working of the commonhold which should be raised. They may include:

- *Details of service charges, outstanding demands and reserve funds.* The percentage contribution for each unit is set out in the commonhold community statement. An in-coming owner will want to be reassured that his share will be fair. Other units can be allocated a 0 percentage, which might be justified because their unit-holders do not have the benefit of the services being funded or might cast an unreasonably heavy burden on the unit being acquired;

- *Enforcement action in relation to the unit* taken by the commonhold association or other unit-holders under the commonhold community statement or the regulations;

- *Compliance with obligations under the statement and the regulations by other unit-holders.* It is important to know whether other unit-holders are in arrears with their service charges, because that could threaten the solvency of the commonhold association. Disputes concerning the use of other units could affect the buyer's enjoyment, disputes about repairs and maintenance could prejudice the stability of his unit;

- *Approval by the association of interests created over other units.* If a unit-holder has been allowed to create a third party interest over his unit, that could impact on the enjoyment of the unit being bought. Perhaps more seriously, the long-term redevelopment prospects of the estate, and with them the value of the unit, could be prejudiced;

- *Mortgages of the common parts.* The financial prospects of the commonhold association may be affected if it has mortgaged all or any of the common parts. Further, the prospect of losing control of that part of the property if the mortgagee realises its security may affect the value of the unit;

- *Claims against the commonhold association.* Contractual or tortious claims by outsiders against the association could threaten its financial stability, although they may be covered by insurance;

- *Observance of the statutory duties in relation to the commonhold association.* If annual returns are not filed, the association would run the risk of being struck off the register of companies;

- *The identity of the directors and secretary* of the commonhold association and the address to which notices should be sent.

Contract

10.19   Normal contractual terms will be appropriate to sell a commonhold unit, although the description of the property should certainly make its status clear. If the property has not yet been built or finished, a unit may be sold by reference to the plan and specifications as is the case with property to be owned in other ways.

10.20   It would not be satisfactory to enter into an agreement to buy a unit in a commonhold which has not yet been established and registered. There would be no unit title and no commonhold community statement. Accordingly, the extent of the unit would not be finalised, nor would there be details of the rights to be enjoyed or obligations to be undertaken. Because of the need to register both the commonhold association at Companies House and the commonhold at the Land Registry, a promoter seeking to sell a prospective unit would not be in a position to offer a firm guarantee that the commonhold would be successfully established.

10.21   The Standard Conditions of Sale (3rd edition) and the Standard Commercial Property Conditions of Sale (1st edition) are appropriate for selling a commonhold unit. The conditions relating to leasehold property will necessarily not apply, but it may be prudent to include a special condition equivalent to condition 8.1.2 of both sets of standard conditions. It could read:

> The seller having provided the buyer with a copy of the commonhold community statement relating to the commonhold of which the

property constitutes a unit, the buyer is treated as entering into the contract knowing and fully accepting its terms.

If the commonhold association has accumulated a sub- **10.22** stantial balance on a reserve fund including contributions from the owner of the unit in question, the seller and buyer will have to consider how this should be dealt with. They are free to make whatever bargain they wish. The provisions governing apportionments in the Standard Conditions of Sale do not apply.

On one view, the balance on a reserve fund is a benefit built **10.23** up by the seller from which the buyer will benefit, because it will reduce his future liabilities. That argues for the buyer making a payment to the seller. The contrary view is that the contributions the seller made to the fund merely paid for the deterioration during his period of ownership. That suggests that the buyer should pay nothing on this account. There is no "correct" answer; the arguments are familiar in connection with assignments of leases.

Transfer

The only documentation needed to complete the transac- **10.24** tion is a transfer of the title to the unit. It may be that a special form of transfer will be prescribed for commonhold units, but the normal form appears to be satisfactory.

Entitlement to membership of the commonhold associa- **10.25** tion will pass automatically to the new unit-holder without documentation. His rights over the common parts arise under the commonhold community statement and will also pass to him automatically once he is entitled to the unit.

Mortgages

A unit-holder is free to mortgage the whole of his unit **10.26** without restriction. The commonhold community state- ment cannot prevent or restrict that power. Limitations on creating other interests in favour of third parties do not apply (s.20(1), (6)(a)). Specifically, the unit-holder does not need the consent of the commonhold association to a mortgage of his unit (s.20(3), (6)(a)). Accordingly, any normal form of mortgage or legal charge may be used.

10.27   Where a commonhold unit is mortgaged "with full title guarantee" or "with limited title guarantee", an additional covenant is implied. The mortgagor covenants that he will fully and promptly observe and perform all his obligations as unit-holder or joint unit-holder under the commonhold community statement (Law of Property (Miscellaneous Provisions) Act 1994, s.5(3A); Sched.5, para.7). This is the equivalent of the additional covenant given when a leasehold is mortgaged, which in that case is that the mortgagor will comply with the lease covenants.

Compulsory purchase

10.28   Necessarily, there is no bar to the compulsory purchase of commonhold land. Exceptionally, it is possible for such an acquisition to apply to part only of a unit without the commonhold association giving consent. The procedure may be the same as for any other compulsory purchase, although there is power to make regulations which may modify it. On completion the land ceases to be commonhold land (s.60).

10.29   The result of partial compulsory purchase could prevent part of the commonhold, or even the whole of the remainder, being viable. Acquisition of part of a unit might make prevent satisfactory occupation of the rest and acquisition of common parts could deprive units of vital facilities. In an extreme case, the acquisition of all the units might, pointlessly, leave the common parts.

10.30   Regulations may be made to allow the commonhold association to intervene to rectify the position. They could allow the association to require the body exercising the compulsory purchase power to acquire the freehold in all or a particular part of the commonhold (s.60(4)(e)). If the regulations are so framed, therefore, they would enable the association to require acquisition of a whole unit instead of only part of it, or of additional land within the common parts so that no isolated and unusable scrap remains.

EFFECT OF TRANSFER

A person acquiring a unit becomes a unit-holder when **10.31** entitled to be registered as proprietor of the freehold (s.12). So the effect of a transfer, whether or not yet registered, is to give the new unit-holder (or in the case of joint unit-holders, all of them separately and jointly: section 13(3)) the rights and duties under the commonhold community statement that the former unit-holder had.

This of course does not apply on a compulsory purchase, **10.32** because the effect of that transfer is that the property ceases to be commonhold land.

No continuing liability

A former unit-holder, who has transferred his unit, has no **10.33** further rights and liabilities. This is, however, without prejudice to any liability incurred or right acquired before the transfer took effect, but it applies even though his name is still registered as proprietor. This effect of a transfer cannot be varied or excluded by contract (s.16(2), (3)). It is the equivalent of the release of a tenant from lease covenants on assigning the whole property (Landlord and Tenant (Covenants) Act 1995, s.5(2)), but there is no equivalent to the saving which excludes assignments by operation of law (1995 Act, s.11(1), (2)).

The corollary of this rule is that the new unit-holder has no **10.34** responsibility for any liability of his predecessor. This simplifies the process of acquiring a unit, because there is no need for enquiries about outstanding debts to the commonhold association, unless a charging order has been registered. Nevertheless, it presents a difficulty in the enforcement of arrears of service charge, which is radically different from the position where a lease changes hands. Because the landlord can threaten to exercise the remedy of forfeiture, arrears are effectively charged on the property. This gives incoming leaseholders an incentive to ensure that arrears have been paid off and can induce mortgagees to settle those debts to safeguard their security.

Chapter 11

Owning a unit

Nature of ownership

11.1 A unit-holder is freehold owner of the unit, which is registered at the Land Registry under a separate title number. In principle, the unit-holder has all the rights and responsibilities of any freeholder. However, they are subject to the terms of the Act, the provisions of the commonhold community statement and, in relation to his membership of the commonhold association, to its memorandum and articles of association.

11.2 In addition, the unit-holder is entitled to such rights over the common parts as may be defined in the commonhold community statement.

11.3 Up to four people may jointly own a commonhold unit (Trustee Act 1925, s.34), but a person under the age of 18 cannot, alone or jointly, own the legal estate in one (Law of

Property Act 1925, ss 19, 20). However, only one joint owner is entitled to be a member of the commonhold association in respect of one unit (Sched.3, para.8).

DISPOSITIONS

Power to lease

It is normally necessary for a unit-holder to obtain the commonhold association's consent before creating an interest over his unit, or the association must be a party to creating it (para. 11.20). This does not apply to mortgaging a unit or granting a lease of one, although there are other restrictions which can apply to leases. **11.4**

The extent of the power to lease a commonhold unit depends on whether or not it is a "residential commonhold unit". A unit comes into this category if the commonhold community statement requires it to be used only for residential purposes or only for those and other incidental purposes (s.17(5)). Presumably, using a garage for car parking would be an "incidental purpose" when considered in connection with a residential flat. On the other hand, where a unit which consists of a shop and a flat, the retail use of the shop is unlikely to be incidental. **11.5**

This will turn on the facts. The commercial use of one room in a residential unit, *e.g.* as an office or a consulting room, would probably be incidental; but where a commercial unit included caretaker's accommodation, the residential use would probably be the incidental one. (See *Cheryl Investments Ltd v. Saldanha*; *Royal Life Saving Society v. Page* [1978] 1 W.L.R. 1329.) **11.6**

A unit-owner can only grant a lease of a residential commonhold unit if it complies with the terms of regulations which have yet to be made. The power to lease residential units is likely to be confined to lettings of up to seven years and to those granted without payment of a premium. An instrument which does not comply with the restrictions is to that extent void (s.17(1)—(3)). **11.7**

The position about a lease granted for someone's life is **11.8** unfortunately complicated. The statutory wording restricting leasing limits the power to create a "term of years absolute". That term, which is defined by the Law of Property Act 1925, s.205(1)(xxvii) and given the same meaning by the Land Registration Act 2002, s.132(1), does not include a lease granted for a life or lives (a lease which is automatically converted into a lease for 90 years, terminable on notice after the death of the person for whose life it was granted: Law of Property Act 1925, s.149(6)). However, a lease of commonhold land is to be "treated as if" it were one converted to a 90 year term and the Act applies accordingly (Sched.5, para.3). That means that if it relates to a residential unit, it is of no effect if that term is longer than the prescribed limit (s.17(3)). In the case of other units, it takes effect subject to any restriction in the commonhold community statement (s.18).

11.9   The fact that people enter into a lease, and pay consideration, perhaps not realising that it is or is partly void, would leave them in an unsatisfactory position. So a party may apply to the court for an order that it take effect as if it provided for a specified form of lease, that money be paid or returned and making such other provision as the court considers appropriate (s.17(4)). If the tenant goes into possession and the lease is treated as valid, he will probably have an implied yearly tenancy (*Martin v. Smith* (1874) 9 L.R. Exch. 50).

11.10 There is no restriction by statute on leases of units which are not residential. But limits may be imposed on the unit-holder's rights by the commonhold community statement (s.18). The Act says that leases "shall have effect subject to any provision of" the statement. Presumably that does not allow the statement to ban leasing altogether. It would be a strange use of language to say that to prevent a lease taking effect at all meant that it was taking effect, albeit subject to the restriction.

Terms of leases

11.11 There is also power, unusually, to make regulations which impose obligations on tenants of units or which allow a commonhold community statement to do so (s.19(1)). In effect, obligations which primarily take effect between the association and a unit-holder, or between two unit-holders, are made to bind a third party. This power might, *e.g.* be used to require tenants to observe user restrictions affecting a unit or to comply with requirements about repairs or about the common parts. Similar obligations can also be imposed on those with matrimonial home rights, under the Family Law Act 1996, over a unit (s.61). In other circumstances, valid restrictive covenants binding the freeholder can be enforced against a tenant (*Hill v. Harris* [1965] 2 Q.B. 601), but the Act's provision extending this to positive covenants is novel.

Regulations can also go much further. They can modify rules of law, whether common law or statutory, about leasehold property. The variations may apply generally, in specific circumstances or to particular types of unit (s.19(4), (5)). This is a very wide ranging power and it is not possible to forecast how it will be used. The extent to which leasing units is feasible and attractive may depend on how it is exercised. **11.12**

The provisions restricting the grant of leases of common- hold units also apply, taking precedence over general rules, in two special cases. A landlord who purports to grant — albeit usually unintentionally — a perpetually renewable lease of a unit is treated as a creating a term of 2,000 years, or a sublease for a fixed term of one day less than the lease out of which it is granted. The validity of that term, under the legislation affecting commonholds, is then judged by the rules set out above. So it is void if it contravenes the regulations or the terms of the commonhold community statement (Law of Property Act 1922, Sched.15, para.5(2), (3); Sched.5, para.1). **11.13**

Similarly, a lease of a unit for a life or lives, or terminable on the tenant's marriage is, under the general law, treated as a grant for 90 years. Its validity then depends on the application of the commonhold rules to that deemed term (Law of Property Act 1925, s.149; Sched.5, para.3) (para. 11.8). **11.14**

Tenant protection

11.15   The various forms of statutory protection for tenants can apply on the letting of a commonhold unit if the conditions which apply are met, and provided that the possibility is not excluded by a regulation varying the law of landlord and tenant (s.19(4)) (para. 11.12).

- *assured shorthold tenancy.* A tenancy of a unit let as a dwelling to an individual as his only or main home will normally be an assured shorthold tenancy. The rent must be over £1,000 a year in Greater London, £250 a year elsewhere, but not over £25,000 a year (Housing Act 1988, Pt I, Chap. 1; Housing Act 1996, s.96; see *Leasehold Law* paras 1.073 *et seq*).

- *secure tenancy.* If a public sector landlord lets a unit to an individual as his only or main home, it will be a secure tenancy unless it falls within certain statutory exceptions (Housing Act 1985, Pt IV; see *Leasehold Law* paras 1.125 *et seq*).

- *business tenancy.* A letting of a unit for occupation by the tenant for business purposes will generally give the tenant renewal rights, subject to specified grounds of opposition by the landlord (Landlord and Tenant Act 1954, Pt II; see *Leasehold Law* paras 1.134 *et seq*).

- *farm business tenancy.* If a unit is farmed commercially a letting of it can constitute a farm business tenancy (Agricultural Tenancies Act 1995; see *Leasehold Law* paras 1.147 *et seq*). This is unlikely to apply because no application may be made to register agricultural land as commonhold land (Sched.2, para.2). However, it is possible that commonhold land could be put to agricultural use at a later date.

Dividing units

11.16   The association must give its written consent (para. 11.23) to a transfer of part only of a unit. Without the consent, the transfer is of no effect (s.21(2)(c), (3)).

11.17   The commonhold system depends on the units remaining

whole and undivided, although formal steps can be taken
to vary these provision in the commonhold community
statement (para. 12.8). For this reason it is not possible to
charge part only of a unit (s.22).

Obviously, it is not possible to guarantee that sufficient   **11.18**
other unit-holders, as members of the commonhold
association, will give their consent (para. 11.23). They
may require a re-negotiation of the percentages in which
service charges are shared, and there may be fundamental
management objections to increasing the number of units.
Changes will require formal amendments to the commonhold community statement and registration formalities. All
this is likely to make a transfer of part of a unit time-
consuming, troublesome and expensive.

The need to maintain the integrity of commonhold units   **11.19**
results in the modification of some general rules. The
power of sale of a mortgagee of a unit does not extend to
the sale of part only of the unit (Law of Property Act 1925,
s.101(1A); Sched.5, para.2). Trustees of land, exercising
their power to partition land between beneficiaries of full
age entitled to trust land in undivided shares, may not
divide a unit (Trusts of Land and Appointment of Trustees
Act 1996, s.7(6); Sched.5, para.8).

Rights over units

A unit-holder who creates an interest, other than a   **11.20**
mortgage or a lease, in his unit the unit-holder must either
have the association's written consent (para. 11.23) or must
make it a consenting party to the transaction. In default,
the instrument or agreement is to that extent void (s.20(3),
(5)).

The reason for requiring the association's agreement is that   **11.21**
one unit-holder's actions may prejudice the value of other
units. Take the example of an easement. If one unit-holder
grants an easement for drainage across his unit to a
neighbour outside the commonhold, the neighbour could

legitimately resist future interference. That could detract from the whole estate's redevelopment prospects.

Commonhold association consent

11.22   The commonhold association's consent, both in the case of a unit-holder who proposes to transfer part of his unit and one who grants an interest in it, must have formal approval.

11.23   The association may only consent, or join in the grant of an interest, if it has passed a resolution to do so. At least 75 per cent of those voting must vote in favour of the resolution (s.20(4)). This seems to be more stringent than requiring 75 per cent of the votes to be cast in favour: a unit-holder who owns more than one unit is entitled on a poll to a vote for each of them, "those who vote" is more appropriate to refer to the number of voters than to the number of votes they cast.

USE AND OCCUPATION

Rights and duties

11.24   The commonhold community statement will deal with some aspects of the use and occupation of a unit. The Act dictates that it must deal with certain topics, although it does not lay down what rules it must make. The duties and obligations specified in the statement will be enforceable under powers in regulations, and may be made to bind tenants and occupiers of the unit with matrimonial home rights (ss. 37(1), 19(1), 61).

11.25   The commonhold community statement regulates the use of a unit (s.14(1)). This will normally specify the only use to which the unit may be put; it could go further, although this seems unlikely (para. 6.11). The statement may also lay down a general prohibition of causing a nuisance or annoyance and possibly other specified behaviour (s.31(5)(h), (i)).

11.26   The statement will also impose duties regarding (s.14(2), (3)):

- insurance (including the use of proceeds to rebuild or reinstate: s.69(2)(a));

- repair and maintenance (including decoration and putting it in sound condition: s.69(2)(b)). The statement might go on to impose a duty to undertake particular works, or to refrain from doing so, including a prohibition on alterations (s.31(5)(b), (g)).

These duties may be imposed either on the unit-holder (or in the case of joint unit-holders, all of them together: s.13(2)) or on the commonhold association and presumably some can be the responsibility of one and some of the other.

There is a wide range of other duties which the Act states that the commonhold community statement can impose, although the list is not exclusive. The matters mentioned are (s.31(5), (6)):   **11.27**

- to pay money, including a provision for interest on late payments;

- to grant access;

- to give notice. A separate provision requires a new unit-holder (or in the case of joint unit-holders, all of them together: s. 13(2)) to give the commonhold association notice of a transfer of a unit (s.15(3));

- to refrain from entering into transactions of a specified kind in relation to the unit. But this cannot apply to a transfer, mortgage or the grant of an interest or charge over the whole unit (ss 15(2), 20(1));

- to indemnify (in the case of joint unit-holders, all of them separately and jointly: s. 13(3)) the commonhold association or another unit-holder against costs arising from breach of a statutory requirement.

It is uncertain how the Party Wall etc. Act 1996 applies to unit-holders. Where a building is built up to or straddles a boundary, that Act gives adjoining owners a series of rights to do work, so long as they comply with the Act's notice and disputes procedure. Two adjoining commonhold units   **11.28** could share a party wall (or a "party structure", which includes a floor partition: 1996 Act, s.20). It is not clear whether a commonhold community statement can restrict the statutory rights conferred by the 1996 Act.

Service charges

11.29 The commonhold community statement specifies the percentage of the commonhold association's expenditure which each unit-holder must pay as a service charge (para. 6.22). It also lays down the percentage contributions to any reserve fund which the association maintains. Regulations may, and presumably will, make provision to enforce payment of service charges. The statement must include provision requiring the unit-holder to pay interest for late payment (ss 31(6), 37).

11.30 Proceedings for debt is the only means of enforcement available. The sums due are not, unlike many leasehold service charges, reserved as rent and therefore it will not be possible to distrain for them. Further, the commonhold community statement cannot impose a sanction for non-payment which involves loss of property (s.31(8)).

11.31 As the service charge payments are not from a tenant to a landlord, the legislation safeguarding tenants by limiting the amount payable to reasonable sums (Landlord and Tenant Act 1985, ss 18—20) does not apply. Were those restrictions to apply, the commonhold association might be in a position where it could not recoup all its expenses so that it faced insolvency. The remedy for unit-holders who consider that the association is spending extravagantly or inappropriately is to exercise their democratic rights as association members to question its management.

11.32 Regulations can be made requiring the tenant of a unit to pay sums to the commonhold association or to a unit-holder (or in the case of joint unit-holders, all of them together: s. 13(2)) which, under the commonhold community statement, are due to be paid by the unit-holder or another tenant of the unit. The payments can be set off against sums the tenant owes and recovered from the unit-holder or another tenant (s.19(2), (3)). The regulations may also require payments from people with matrimonial home rights over the unit (s.61).

It is not entirely clear how this will operate, but it seems likely to provide a machinery to allow the commonhold association to collect service charges, payable by a unit-holder, directly from his tenant. This would be comparable to the Law of Distress Amendment Act 1908, s.6, which allows a head landlord to collect rent directly from a sub-tenant. The convenience of this is clear in the case of an absentee unit-holder/landlord, but it may raise difficulties on the unit-holder's bankruptcy. **11.33**

ENFORCING OBLIGATIONS

An obligation which the commonhold community state-ment imposes on a unit-holder will be made enforceable by regulations (s.37(1)). They can require a defaulter to pay compensation, in which case they will make provision for determining the amount of it and for interest on late payment (s.37(3)). There will be no distinction between those of a positive nature and those which are restrictive, so that the general law difficulties in enforcing positive covenants will, within a commonhold, disappear. **11.34**

Regulations may also be made to ensure that regulations are complied with whoever occupies a unit. They may allow the commonhold community statement to impose obligations directly on a tenant of a unit (s.19(1)(b)). In this context, tenant is to be read as including a person with matrimonial home rights (s.61), so a unit-holder's spouse in occupation of a residential unit would also be bound. **11.35**

The directors of the commonhold association have a duty to enforce the obligations imposed on the owners and occupiers of a unit. However, the Act directs them to take account of certain other factors (para. 9.5). **11.36**

Chapter 12

Varying a commonhold

When arising

12.1 There are five distinct circumstances in which there may be changes to the fundamental arrangements made for a commonhold.

- There may be an application to enlarge the commonhold;

- The unit-holders may wish to vary the extent of constituent parts of the commonhold, either a unit or the common parts;

- They may want to make other changes to the ownership terms;

- It may be necessary to rectify a document which does not to comply with the Act;

- Land may have been registered as commonhold land in error.

There is also the exceptional case of a developer cancelling **12.2** the registration of a commonhold without unit-holders during the transitional period, so that the commonhold never comes into operation (para. 5.77). That is not dealt with here.

ENLARGEMENT

Application

To enlarge a commonhold by adding more land, a further **12.3** registration application must be made to the Land Registry. The freeholder of the additional land must make it (s.2). The concurrence of others is generally required in two ways. First, the application must be accompanied any necessary consents, relating to the extra land, in the same way as the original application (s.41(5)(a)) (para. 5.38). Secondly, the approval of a resolution of the commonhold association, passed unanimously (*i.e. nem. con.*: s.36(5)) is normally needed before an application is made to the Land Registry to register the additional land (s.41(3), (4)).

There is one exception to the requirement of a resolution of **12.4** the commonhold association, which is for the benefit of a developer. Clearly, until the end of the transitional period (para. 7.3) of a registration without unit-holders, a resolution of the commonhold association is meaningless because no unit has been disposed of. But once that period has ended, the unit-holders might block the addition of land unless the developer had an overriding power. He can be given that power, so that no resolution is needed, provided the commonhold community statement makes that clear (s.58(3)(d)). That gives the developer the power, at his discretion, to increase the size of the commonhold before he completes his work. This allows him to hold back land in case the demand for units is disappointing, and then add it later. Or he can start the development while he is still negotiating to acquire additional land.

12.5 The following must also be submitted with the registration application for the additional land (s.41(5)(b), (c)):

- An application to register an amended commonhold community statement, covering both the existing commonhold land and the added land;

- A certificate by the directors of the commonhold association covering two points. First, it certifies that the applying association has passed the necessary resolution (except, presumably, if the developer is applying and no resolution is needed). Secondly, it states that the added land is not land for which an application for registration as commonhold land is precluded (para 5.17).

12.6 If all the extra land is to be added to the common parts, the commonhold association will immediately be entitled to be registered as proprietor and the Land Registry is to register the association without an application. So far as the rights and duties in the commonhold community statement apply to the added land, they come into force on registration (s.41(7)).

12.7 If the extra land is to constitute or include additional units, the provisions applying to a registration without unit-holders or a registration with unit-holders, as the case may be, apply to the added land as they applied to the original land.

CONSTITUENT PARTS

Unit

12.8 One or more unit-holder may want to redefine the extent of the property included in his or their units. The purpose may be either to remove land from one unit and add it to another — in which case, the extent of both units is amended — or land may be taken from a unit to add it to the common parts. A unit-holder only has the power voluntarily to dispose of a part of his unit if he has the consent of the commonhold association (para. 11.16). This will involve amending the commonhold community statement. So a simple transfer of part, splitting a unit into two, does not avoid the formalities for changing the size of a unit or the common parts or for reducing the size of the commonhold by a transfer to an outside owner.

A proposed amendment to a commonhold community **12.9** statement to redefine the extent of a unit — whether extending it or reducing its size — may only be made with the consent of both the unit-holder and of the proprietor of any registered charge. That consent must be given in writing before the amendment is made. Regulations may give the power to dispense with consent in prescribed circumstances (ss 23, 24(2), (3), 30(1)—(3)).

The effect on a registered charge of varying the extent of a **12.10** unit on which it is secured is laid down by the Act. If land is added to the unit, the charge is automatically extended to include the extra property. If the size of the unit is reduced, the charge is extinguished in so far as it applies to the land excluded. Regulations may require notice of what has happened to be given to the Land Registry, so that the register may reflect the changes (s.24).

Common parts

Where a unit is reduced in size to add land to the common **12.11** parts, the commonhold association is automatically entitled to be registered as proprietor of the freehold of that additional land. The association is to be registered by the Land Registry without the need for any application (s.30(4)).

The provisions set out above then apply (para. 12.6).

The commonhold association may dispose of its freehold **12.13** estate in any of the common parts. The commonhold community statement may not prohibit or restrict that power (s.27).

If the commonhold association disposes of land in the **12.14** common parts to a unit-holder, to add to his unit, this would be an increase in the size of the unit for which the formalities are dealt with above (para. 12.7). If the disposal was to someone outside the commonhold, the land would cease to be "land in relation to which a commonhold exercises functions", which is the definition of commonhold land (s.1(2)). The land would therefore cease to be commonhold land.

OTHER OWNERSHIP TERMS

Commonhold community statement

12.15 It is possible to change the terms laid down by the commonhold community statement. This may be needed following a redefinition of the units, *e.g.* the unit-holders may agree that the service charge proportions should be varied. Or, the change may arise independently, *e.g.* a decision to change the responsibility for insurance from individual unit-holders to the commonhold association or vice versa.

12.16 Every statement must, as provided by regulations, make provision about how it may be amended (s.33(1)). Presumably, the regulations will lay down requirements to be follows. The prescribed formalities must be observed. The amendment only takes effect when registered at the Land Registry (s.33(3)).

12.17 It is not yet clear what preliminary consultation process or consents will be required before a commonhold community statement is amended. However, it should be noted that, as well as unit-holders and the commonhold association, tenants of units may be affected because regulations may allow obligations to be placed directly on them (s.19(1)).

Registration

12.18 The following must accompany an application to register an amended commonhold community statement (s.33(5)—(7)):

- a certificate by the directors of the commonhold

association that the amended statement satisfies the Act's requirements;

- when the extent of a unit is redefined, any necessary consent or a court order dispensing with it;

- when the extent of the common parts is changed, any necessary consent or a court order dispensing with it.

After registration, the Land Registry retains the amended **12.19** statement. It is referred to on the register in place of the original version (s.33(4)).

RECTIFICATION

Court declaration

The court has power to make a declaration which will **12.20** in effect require rectification of the memorandum and articles of association of the commonhold association and/ or of the commonhold community statement. If the effect is that the commonhold comes to an end, the court has the same powers as on a winding-up (s.55) (para. 14.7).

A unit owner (or in the case of joint unit-holders, all of **12.21** them or any of them separately: s. 13(3)) may apply to the court for a declaration in relation to one or both of the documents. There is a time limit for applying. Unless the court gives permission to extend time, the applicant must apply within three months of becoming unit-holder or within three months of the document's failure to comply with relevant requirement (s.40(1), (4)).

The grounds for applying for a declaration differ slightly **12.22** (s.40(1)):

- In the case of the memorandum and articles association, the contention must be that they do not comply with the regulations which lay down their form and content (Sched.3, para.2(1)).

- In the case of the commonhold community statement, the contention must be that they do not comply with a requirement imposed by the Act or by virtue of it, *i.e.* by regulations.

12.23 When the court makes a declaration, it may make whatever order appears appropriate. This can include requiring an officer of the commonhold association to amend the document or to take specified steps, awarding compensation and providing that land cease to be commonhold land. There is a time limit for applying (s.40(2), (3)).

REGISTRATION IN ERROR

Court application

12.24 If land is mistakenly registered in a commonhold, the error must be corrected by a court order. The registrar's power to order an alteration of the register (Land Registration Act 2002, Sched.4) does not apply. This covers cases where the registration application does not comply with the statutory requirements, where the commonhold association directors' certificate was inaccurate and where the registration contravened the Act's requirements (s.6(1), (2)).

12.25 A person who claims to have been adversely affected by the registration may apply to a court (the High Court, a county court or a tribunal: s.66) for a declaration that the freehold should not have been registered as a commonhold. A court making a declaration may make any order which it considers appropriate.

12.26 An order may include confirming or rectifying the register, that the land cease to be commonhold land, requiring that documents be amended, that an individual pay compensation, or applying, disapplying or modifying the provisions for indemnity by the Land Registry (Land Registration Act 2002, Sched.8) (s.6(3)—(6)).

Chapter 13

Particular parties

INTERESTS IN A UNIT

Mortgagees

The formalities and documentation for taking a mortgage on a commonhold unit are the same as for taking a mortgage of other freehold land. When leasehold property is mortgaged, particularly in the case of a flat, the existence of a management or landlord company of which the leaseholder is a member, may require additional care. It is sometimes necessary to make particular arrangements to ensure that, if the mortgagee exercises the power of sale, the buyer can become a shareholder. No equivalent action is needed when taking a mortgage of a commonhold unit. The commonhold association is a company without a share

13.1

capital and entitlement to membership follows ownership of the unit (s.34(1), Sched.3, para. 7).

13.2 A mortgage of a commonhold unit offers virtually the same security as in the case of other property. In certain respects it is reinforced by the Act, although there are two modifications which might be prejudicial.

13.3 There are two possible drawbacks. First, in enforcing the security, the mortgagee is not entitled to sell part only of a unit unless the commonhold association consents (Sched.5, para.2) (para. 11.17). Secondly, he is bound by the restrictions on leasing which apply to the unit.

13.4 On the other hand, there are rules to ensure that the mortgagee's interests are not subverted. His consent is required before the size of a unit can be reduced and if a mortgaged unit is enlarged the extra land is added to the security (s.24(2), (5)). The commonhold community statement cannot contain any provision equivalent to a forfeiture provision in a lease (s.31(8)). So, in contrast to the position where the security is leasehold property, the mortgagee is not at risk and does not need a right to relief.

13.5 The covenants for title implied into the mortgage, if it is expressed to be granted "with full title guarantee" or "with limited title guarantee", include a mortgagor's covenant to observe and perform all his obligations under the commonhold community statement (Law of Property (Miscellaneous Provisions) Act 1994, s.5(3A); Sched.5, para.7(3)). This will generally be considered sufficient protection for the mortgagee, who is unlikely to want to participate in the management of the commonhold.

13.6 However, there may be strategic management decisions where the mortgagee would wish to influence or dictate the way in which the mortgagor votes in his capacity as a member of the commonhold association. This could apply, *e.g.* to decisions to sell off common parts to raise a capital sum, to lease them to raise an income which would reduce service charges, to mortgage them or to wind-up the association. There is no reason why a mortgagee should not require the mortgagee to execute an irrevocable power of attorney (Powers of Attorney Act 1971, s.4) authorising him to act on the mortgagor's behalf at general meetings of the association.

For the full protection of the mortgagee, the unit-holder **13.7** would also have to contract not to vote personally, as the grant of a power of attorney would not of itself prevent his doing so. A power delegating the right to vote could be limited. It could apply to voting on resolutions of a certain nature, assuming they could be unambiguously identified, or on resolutions of which the mortgagee gave notice. Either way, the mortgagor would have to be obliged to give the mortgagee copies of all notices of meetings, which could generate a good deal of unwanted paper. In Australia, there are statutory powers of this type, but they are largely disregarded by mortgagees.

On a voluntary winding-up of the commonhold associa- **13.8** tion, the freehold of all the units is transferred to the association (s.49(2)). This is something which a mortgagee cannot prevent, except to the extent that special contractual arrangements have been made. However, the transfer of the unit would be subject to the mortgage. The mortgagee would therefore retain the security and the mortgagor's covenant to pay would not be affected.

When realising its security on the mortgagor's default, a **13.9** mortgagee will be well advised to exercise its power of sale, rather than taking possession. If the mortgagee itself becomes the unit-holder, it may well incur further liabilities personally. If the unit continues in the name of the mortgagor, and the mortgagee does not put itself into the position of "being entitled to be registered as proprietor" this is avoided.

Developers

In carrying out new leasehold developments, developers **13.10** have become accustomed to making arrangements which ensure that they do not lose control until all the leases have been sold. If the leaseholders are to become members of a company which they will control, the developer generally ensures that he keeps voting control during the marketing period. Similar arrangements are possible when developing a commonhold.

13.11 The commonhold community statement may, subject to regulations to be made, make provision to require unit-holders to co-operate with the developer and to allow land to be added to the commonhold without an approving resolution of the commonhold association (s.58(2), (3)). Also, during a transitional period, the developer can be a member of the association (Sched.3, para.6(3)).

13.12 Although there are provisions for adding further land to an established commonhold, the Act's arrangements are unlikely to be adequate for a substantial development, built in phases. All the land ultimately to be included in the commonhold can however be registered as part of it immediately, so that it is not a question of later enlargement.

13.13 A large estate may have to be developed over a long period and the plans for later stages may not be settled at the outset. If, *e.g.* it were not possible to say at the outset how many units there would be and what services they would require, it would be difficult to be sufficiently definite in drawing up the initial documentation. There are provisions for amending commonhold community statements, but it is not yet clear what their scope will be and how they will work. The safest course may be to assume that larger commonhold developments will have to wait for follow-up legislation when the system has become established.

Tenants

13.14 A tenant of a commonhold unit, or part of a unit, enjoys the normal legal estate for a term of years, provided that (in the case of a residential unit) the letting complies with the conditions laid down by regulations. To this there is one exception. The tenant of part of a unit cannot validly charge his lease: the prohibition of charging part only of a unit is not restricted to a charge over the freehold (s.22(1)).

13.15 If a residential unit is let on terms which do not comply with the conditions which the regulations prescribe, the instrument or agreement purporting to grant let it is of no effect (s.17). Nevertheless, as between the landlord (*i.e.* the unit-holder) and the tenant, there will presumably be a tenancy by estoppel (*Mackley v. Nutting* [1949] 2 K.B. 55), but that is not binding on third parties (*Tadman v. Henman* [1893] 2 Q.B. 168). Accordingly, in such a case the tenant would not be able to maintain any claim against other unit-holders or the commonhold association, *e.g.* on a winding-up.

In normal circumstances, however, a tenant will probably **13.16** be able to enforce duties which are owed by another tenant, by the unit-holder or by the commonhold association. That would go beyond the powers which a tenant would have under the general law, but regulations may make such provision (s.37(2)(g)), and they are likely to do so.

It is generally prudent for a tenant of property not in a **13.17** commonhold to inspect his landlord's title, if only because he will be bound by restrictive covenants which affect the freehold (*Hill v. Harris* [1956] 2 Q.B. 601). When taking a lease of commonhold land, the tenant should also inspect a copy of the commonhold community statement. There is power to make him bound by the obligations in the statement, whether positive or negative (s.19(1)).

The legal position of a tenant of a commonhold unit is not **13.18** yet certain. There is a very wide power to make regulations to modify the rules, whether common law or statutory, which would otherwise apply (s.19(4)). This power can be used to reduce tenants' rights and the safeguards which would otherwise apply, although conversely tenants may be given additional rights. Until it is clear what changes, if any, will be made, it is not possible to advise prospective tenants definitively.

Subject to that major proviso, that regulations may vary **13.19** the established rules, it must be assumed that:

- a letting of a residential unit will be an assured tenancy, provided the normal qualifications are met (Housing Act 1988, s.1). Further, when the letting is for less than seven years, the unit-holder as landlord will be responsible for structural and outside repairs (Landlord and Tenant Act 1985, ss 13, 14);

- a letting of a commercial or industrial unit will give the tenant the qualified statutory right to a new tenancy when it expires (Landlord and Tenant Act 1954, s.24).

FIDUCIARIES

Trustees

13.20 Trustees are generally authorised to acquire freehold land, for investment, the occupation of a beneficiary or for other reasons. Exceptions are where the trust instrument prohibits it, where the trust consists of or includes settled land or the Universities and College Estates Act 1925 applies (Trustee Act 2000, ss 8—10). Accordingly, trustees are authorised to buy a commonhold unit, although because of the restrictions on leasing it will not always make a suitable investment.

13.21 Trustees who buy a unit for a beneficiary to occupy may well not wish to be concerned with day-to-day issues relating to the management of the commonhold. To avoid this, they can to delegate their relevant powers to the occupying beneficiary by power of attorney (Trusts of Land and Appointment of Trustees Act 1996, s.9).

13.22 Trustees of land have powers to partition land between beneficiaries of full age who are entitled to the trust land in undivided shares. These powers are modified in one respect. They may not divide a commonhold unit unless they have written consent from the commonhold association (Trusts of Land and Appointment of Trustees Act 1996, s.7(6); Sched.5, para.8).

Charities

13.23 Charitable trustees also have the trustees' statutory power to invest in land, so they are permitted to acquire commonhold units. But there may only be limited circumstances in which this is appropriate. The restrictions on letting residential units (s.17) may make them unsuitable as income producing investments. Units might nevertheless be acquired to further the objects of a charity in providing housing accommodation.

Personal representatives

Personal representatives of a deceased unit-holder will themselves become unit-holders when they are entitled to be registered as proprietors of the unit, presumably on the grant of representation. This will make them liable for the outgoings of the unit, if they have not already become responsible. **13.24**

On the transfer of a unit, which includes a transfer on death by operation of law (s.15(1)), the incoming unit-holder becomes responsible for all the associated liabilities as soon as he is entitled to be registered (s.12) even if he is not yet registered as proprietor (s.16(1), (4)). This may mean that an executor becomes liable from the date of the deceased's death, so long as he does not renounce his right to probate. The executor would no doubt be entitled to be indemnified from the deceased's estate, but if the estate were heavily indebted this could be a factor in deciding whether to renounce. **13.25**

Trustees in bankruptcy

A unit which forms part of a bankrupt's estate will vest in the trustee in bankruptcy when he is appointed or, in the case of the official receiver, when he becomes trustee (Insolvency Act 1986, s.306). He will thereupon become entitled to be registered as proprietor of the freehold estate in the unit, and therefore unit-holder. **13.26**

Having regard to any outstanding mortgage and ongoing liabilities, the trustee may conclude that it is not to the creditors' advantage for him to hold the unit. If a mortgagee does not sell it, to realise its security, the trustee may treat it as onerous property and exercise his right to disclaim it. If the unit is a dwelling house, the trustee must give notice to everyone occupying it, or claiming a right to do so, before disclaiming (Insolvency Act 1986, ss 315, 318). **13.27**

13.28 A person who suffers loss or damage as a result of a disclaimer may prove for it in the bankruptcy (Insolvency Act 1986, s.315(5)). Presumably, this would give the commonhold association a right to prove for consequential loss.

Attorneys

13.29 As an owner of freehold land, a unit-holder is entitled to appoint an attorney to act on his behalf, either generally or to carry out specific functions. If he wants to give his attorney general powers, he can do so with the statutory form of power (Powers of Attorney Act 1971, Sched.1). There is no time limit on the period for which such a power can remain effective, unless the power itself imposes one. However, once it is more than a year old, those dealing with the attorney may require a declaration that the attorney has had no notice of any event revoking the power (to trigger the provisions for the protection of third parties in section 5 of the 1971 Act).

13.30 A unit-holder may also execute an enduring power of attorney (Enduring Powers of Attorney Act 1985, s.1). This enables the attorney to continue to act after the unit-holder ceases to have mental capacity, provided that the attorney complies with registration formalities at the Court of Protection.

13.31 If a unit is jointly owned, different provisions may apply when one of the joint unit-holders wishes to appoint an attorney. So long as the unit-holder continues to have a beneficial interest in the unit, he can act as he would have done had he been the sole owner. Any power which he grants then continues in force as it otherwise would have done so long as he retains some beneficial interest.

13.32 A joint unit-holder who is a trustee, and is not entitled to a beneficial interest, is limited to granting a power of attorney for no more than 12 months (Trustee Act 1925, s.25). He can use the statutory short form of trustee power of attorney (1925 Act, s.25(6); Trustee Delegation Act 1999, s.5(1)).

Visitors

A visitor to a commonhold unit will have the usual rights **13.33**
of a licensee. However, there is a material difference
between a leasehold and a commonhold development in
the protection offered to visitors who are injured as a result
of a defect in the premises. In the case of leasehold
property, the landlord, as well as the tenant, owes a duty of
care to visitors. This applies to a landlord who knows or
"ought to in all the circumstances to have known of the
relevant defect" (Defective Premises Act 1972, s.4). As a
commonhold unit is freehold, and the commonhold
association is in no sense the landlord, someone injured
because of a defect in the unit can only have a right of
action against the unit-holder.

The responsibility to anyone injured on the common parts **13.34**
will rest with the commonhold association, in which they
are vested. It will generally be important, for the protection
of the interests of all the unit-holders that the association
should insure against such claims. Liability would otherwise fall on the unit-holders through their service charges.
They will avoid liability for a major claim if the association
becomes insolvent and is wound-up, because as members
of the company they have limited liability. However, if the
association has accumulated reserves, including a reserve
fund established for a limited purpose, they would be put
towards paying off the general liabilities on a winding-up
(s.56).

Neighbours

How the law affects the relations between a unit-holder **13.35**
and his neighbour depends in part whether the neighbour is
a fellow unit-holder in the same commonhold. In non-
property matters, however, normal principles apply. So,
e.g. the law of nuisance applies to restrain both owners
from using their property in a way which cause a nuisance
to the other.

Rights and obligations between fellow unit-holders are **13.36**

largely governed by the commonhold community statement. That lays down the use to which each unit may be
put and details easements and any other rights enjoyed by
unit-holders over other property within the commonhold.
Enforcement is the subject of regulations made under the
Act (s.37). A defaulter may have to pay compensation.

13.37   Between a unit-holder and a neighbouring land owner
outside the commonhold, normal rules generally apply.
The enforcement of restrictive covenants depends on the
normal equitable rules and positive covenants will not be
directly enforceable against successors in title. Easements
which existed before the commonhold was established, and
which are registered if required, will continue. A unit-
holder can presumably acquire an easement over adjoining
property outside the commonhold. A unit-holder who
wishes to grant a new easement to a neighbour needs the
consent of the commonhold association (s.20(3)).

13.38   It is uncertain how the Party Wall etc., Act 1996 will apply
within a commonhold. That Act gives a property owner a
series of unequivocal rights in relation to walls and other
boundary features dividing properties in different ownership ("A building owner shall have the following rights
...": 1996 Act, s.2(2)), subject only to complying with a
notice and dispute resolution procedure. It is not clear how
any conflict between these rights and any prohibition in the
commonhold community statement will be resolved.

Squatters

13.39   How the rules about the acquisition of title by adverse
possession affect commonhold is not clear. The matter is
complicated by the reforms introduced by the Land
Registration Act 2002. In relation to registered land, and
all commonhold land must be registered, no limitation
period is to run and title is no longer to be extinguished at
the expiry of the limitation period (Limitation Act 1980, ss
15, 17; Land Registration Act 2002, s.96). But a squatter
can still acquire title.

13.40   Until now, the effect of acquiring a registered title by
adverse possession was that the registered proprietor held

the property in trust for the new owner. When satisfied that title had been acquired by an applicant for registration, the registrar was obliged to transfer it to the new owner (Land Registration Act 1925, s.75). Where title has already been acquired by adverse possession by the date on which the Land Registration Act 2002 takes effect, those provisions continue to apply for a transitional period of three years (Land Registration Act 2002, Sched.12, para.18).

The new provisions entitle someone who has been in adverse possession for ten years to apply for registration. If the application is contested, there are only limited grounds on which it can succeed. Title, therefore, passes if and when the register is amended, and there is no trust in favour of the squatter (Land Registration Act 2002, Sched 6). **13.41**

In relation to a commonhold unit, both sets of rules raise a number of questions which for the moment remain unanswered: **13.42**

- If a squatter acquires title to part only of a unit, which may well happen in the case of a unit consisting of two or more separate parcels, what is the impact of the rule that a unit must be dealt with as an integral whole unless the commonhold association consents (para.11.17)?

- Is there a distinction between adverse possession by another unit-holder, where one might expect the land in question to be added to his unit even though that would involve a variation of the commonhold community statement, and adverse possession by an outsider?

- When exactly does the former owner cease to be the unit-holder so that the squatter is substituted? A unit-holder is the person "entitled to be registered as the proprietor of the freehold estate in the unit" (s.12). In relation to the commonhold association, "where a member ceases to be a unit-holder ... (a) he shall cease to be a member" (Sched.3, para.12). The date of transfer therefore not only affects liability for such matters as service charges, it may also determine the validity of a winding-up resolution which purports to be passed unanimously (s.44).

13.43   Similar questions arise when someone, whether a unit-holder or not, occupies part of the common parts by adverse possession.

13.44   The Act provides no answer to these questions. But presumably, at least so far as adverse possession by a unit-holder is concerned, they cannot arise in practice until the commonhold legislation has been in force for ten years and the first difficulties are likely to present themselves later than that. There is, therefore, time for amending legislation if that is needed.

Chapter 14

Ending a commonhold

Contents

OVERVIEW

Ways to end commonhold

There is a variety of ways in which a commonhold may come to an end. Some finish the whole development, others remove particular land from the commonhold. It is, however, a principle of this statute-introduced system that it can only end in one of the ways prescribed in the Act.

14.1

The ways in which a commonhold may come to an end are:

14.2

• Voluntary winding-up of the commonhold association.

This necessarily brings the commonhold to an end;

- Compulsory winding-up of the commonhold association by the court. However, even though the association is liquidated, the commonhold can in some circumstances continue;

- Voluntary withdrawal by a developer who applied to register a commonhold without unit-holders (para. 5.76). He only has the right to do this during the transitional period, before he has disposed of any individual unit;

- As a result of the compulsory purchase of some or all of the land (para. 10.28). The land which is compulsorily acquired ceases to be commonhold land. The purchase may directly end the commonhold or the commonhold association may require the acquiring body to take the remainder of the commonhold land;

- Cancellation of a registration made in error (para. 7.14);

- Rectification of either the memorandum and articles of association of the commonhold association or of the commonhold community statement (para. 12.20).

Winding-up: property consequences

14.3   The Act treats the ending a commonhold as a question of winding-up the commonhold association. Property owners must, therefore, fit their objectives into the company winding-up framework. If they intend to reorganise the development on a leasehold basis, to change to single ownership of the entire property or dispose of it for redevelopment, voluntary winding-up will normally be appropriate. This assumes that the association is solvent, but that a commonhold is no longer needed or appropriate. What the unit-holders intend in relation to future ownership of the property is spelled out in the termination statement (para. 14.14).

14.4   There is a fundamental property difference between a voluntary and a compulsory winding-up. If it is voluntary, the commonhold association automatically becomes entitled to be registered proprietor of the freehold in all the units (s.49(3)). That obviously is a temporary situation, and is pending implementation of the termination statement. But it demonstrates that the whole development is unified and ready to be dealt with. Or, if it is to be divided, the boundaries between the different parts need no longer be those between the former units.

The association may be insolvent, but the unit-holders may not want to wind-up the development. The management of the association may have been incompetent and financially inept. All the same, the unit-holders may be content with the properties which they own and occupy and may wish to continue to do so. In these circumstances they will want a successor association to take over running the commonhold, leaving the original association to be wound-up. They achieve this by seeking a succession order (para. 14.32). Obviously, the creditors of the old association may be far from content to see the unit-holders walk away from the association's debts while continuing to benefit from their units. A compromise may have to be negotiated.   **14.5**

The association's assets do not include any interest in the units: so that part of the property is not available to pay the debts. However, the continuing value of the units may well depend on the availability of the common parts, for access, services, etc. and the common parts are assets of the association. The interdependence emphasises the importance of working for a mutually acceptable solution.   **14.6**

Commonhold ceasing

When a commonhold comes to an end as a result of the cancellation of a registration made in error or of the rectification of documents, the court has the same powers as it has on making a winding-up order (s.55(1), (2)).   **14.7**

This means that a liquidator can be appointed and if he is, he has the powers of one appointed for the purposes of a winding-up order made under section 125 of the Insolvency Act 1986 (s.55(3)). The functions of a liquidator are to get in the assets, realise them, pay the creditors and distribute   **14.8** any surplus to those entitled (1986 Act, s.143(1)). If the court makes an order that the land cease to be commonhold land, it can direct that the liquidator exercise his powers in a particular way or vary his rights and duties (s.55(4)).

COMPANY LIQUIDATION RULES

14.9 The Act makes some express provision about winding-up commonhold associations. Where there is no special provision, the general rules concerning company liquidation apply, because the association is a company incorporated under the Companies Acts.

Definitions

14.10 The Act uses a number of terms which are also employed in the Insolvency Act 1986. It expressly adopts the definitions from the 1986 Act:

- *Declaration of solvency.* A statutory declaration by all the directors of the association (or of a majority if more than two) that after full inquiry they consider that the association will be able to pay its debts in full (s.43(2); 1986 Act, s.89).

- *Liquidator.* In a voluntary winding-up, the liquidator is appointed by the association in general meeting (s.44(4); 1986 Act, s.91(1)). A liquidator must be a person who is qualified as an insolvency practitioner (1986 Act, s.230(3)). For the qualifications for acting as an insolvency practitioner, see 1986 Act, s.390.

- *Winding-up resolution.* An association's resolution in general meeting to wind up counts as "a resolution for voluntary winding-up", which covers both cases of solvent and insolvent liquidation (s.44(3)); 1986 Act, s.84(1), (2)). A copy of a resolution must be sent within 15 days to the Registrar of Companies and notice of it must be published in the *London Gazette* (1986 Act, ss 84(3), 85).

- *Winding-up order.* A winding-up order is the court's

order on a winding-up petition (s.50(2)(c); 1986 Act, s.125).

The Act also defines a *termination-statement resolution* (s.43(2)). This is a resolution of the commonhold association approving the terms of termination statement (para. 14.14). **14.11**

SOLVENT WINDING-UP

Voluntary winding-up

A voluntary winding-up of a commonhold association requires the agreement of at least 80 per cent of its members. However, if all the members agree there is a streamlined procedure cutting out the need for one application to the court. The normal list of circumstances in which a company may be voluntarily wound up (Insolvency Act 1986, s.84) apply to commonhold associations, but subject to the provisions of the Act (Sched.5, para.6). **14.12**

In outline, the voluntary winding-up procedure is: **14.13**

- Prepare a termination statement.
- Pass a termination-statement resolution.
- Make a declaration of insolvency.
- Pass a winding-up resolution.
- Appoint a liquidator.
  - * *80 per cent agreement cases only:* Apply to court for an order determining the terms and conditions for making a termination application and the terms of the termination statement to accompany it.
- Make a termination application.

Termination statement

The termination statement makes proposals for the distribution of assets. This relates both to the association's assets and to all the freehold land in the commonhold. Of **14.14**

course, the units — as distinct from the common parts —
are not the property of the association, but the effect of the
termination application with which the winding-up ends is
to vest the units in the association (s.49(3)). This means
that the winding-up can facilitate a sale for redevelopment.
If the objective is that the units remain owned by the unit-
holders, the statement can propose that they be re-vested.

14.15   The commonhold community statement may have made
advance arrangements for winding-up, by requiring
particular provisions to be made in the termination
statement. In that event, those arrangements must be
adopted. However, any member of the association may
apply for a court order that they be disapplied, whether
generally, in specified matters or for a specified purpose
(s.47).

14.16   The termination statement must be adopted by a resolution
of the commonhold association, passed with at least 80 per
cent of the members voting in favour (s.43(1)(b), (c)). This
is the termination-statement resolution.

Declaration of solvency

14.17   The directors' declaration of solvency (para. 14.10) must be
made during the five weeks before the winding-up
resolution is passed and it must be filed at Companies
House within the 15 days after the passing of the resolution
(Insolvency Act 1986, s.89(2), (3)).

Winding-up resolution

14.18   Members of a commonhold association who wish to wind
it up voluntarily must pass a winding-up resolution. The
association must pass it in general meeting. Either, it can
be passed unanimously, with 100 per cent of members
voting in favour; not just 100 per cent of the members
voting, *i.e.* true unanimity. Or, the resolution can be passed
by a majority of at least 80 per cent of members voting in
favour (ss 44(1)(a), 45(1)(a)).

Liquidator

The commonhold association, in general meeting, must also appoint a liquidator (ss 44(1)(b), 45(1)(b)). When it has done so, all the powers of the directors cease, unless the liquidator or the association in general meeting agree otherwise (Insolvency Act 1986, s.91(2)). **14.19**

The liquidator has to notify the Land Registry of his appointment (s.48(2)). **14.20**

Termination application

The final step in the winding-up is for the liquidator to make a termination application to the Land Registry. It must be accompanied by the termination statement (s.46(2)). **14.21**

In a case where the winding-up resolution was passed unanimously, the termination application can be made within six months after the resolution was passed (s.44(2)). If the liquidator fails to apply during that period, a unit-holder — or someone within a class of persons yet to be prescribed by regulation — can do so (s.44(3)). **14.22**

Where the winding-up resolution was passed unanimously, the liquidator must consider the provisions of the termination statement as soon as possible. If he is content with the statement, he must inform the Land Registry. Otherwise, he has a duty to apply to the court to determine the terms of the statement (Insolvency Act 1986, s.112), and send a copy of the court's determination both to the Land Registry and to Companies House (s.48). **14.23**

If the winding-up resolution was passed by an affirmative vote of at least 80 per cent of the members but was not unanimous, there is a two stage procedure (s.45(2), (3)): **14.24**

- First, the liquidator has a period — yet to be prescribed — during which he must apply to the court for an order to specify the terms and conditions on which the termination application may be made and what should be the terms of the termination statement to accompany it;

- Secondly, during the three months following that order, the liquidator must resolve to make a termination application. At least 50 per cent of its members must vote in favour.

Again, if the liquidator defaults, a unit-holder, or someone in a prescribed class, may make either of the applications (s.45(4)).

14.25 The final step in the winding-up is the termination application. The association applies to the Land Registry that the land specified in its memorandum of association should cease to be commonhold land.

14.26 The liquidator has to notify the Land Registry of his appointment and must consider the termination statement as soon as possible. If he is content with it, he must inform the Land Registry. Otherwise, he has a duty to apply to the court to determine the terms of the statement, and send a copy of the court's determination to the Land Registry (s.48).

14.27 When the Land Registry is notified that the liquidator is content with the termination statement, or the court has determined its terms, the association becomes entitled to be registered as proprietor of every unit (s.49).

Summary

14.28 This chart summarises the two voluntary winding-up procedures:

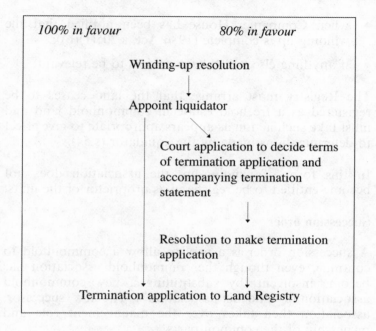

100% in favour   _80% in favour_

Winding-up resolution

↓

Appoint liquidator

Court application to decide terms
of termination application and
accompanying termination
statement

↓

Resolution to make termination
application

Termination application to Land Registry

INSOLVENT WINDING-UP

Compulsory winding-up

A petition may be presented to the court to wind-up the   **14.29**
commonhold association. Although it will most often be
creditors who petition, the company itself or the directors
may do so. Also, a member may petition on the ground
that the company cannot pay its debts or that it is just and
equitable to wind it up. Finally, the Secretary of State may
take action following a report by inspectors (Insolvency
Act 1986, ss 122(1)(f), (g), 124).

On hearing the petition, the court has the option of making   **14.30**
a succession order (s.51(1)) (para. 14.32). If it does not do
so, the liquidator must as soon as possible notify the Land
Registry:

* that no succession order was made;

* of any directions given by the court (Insolvency Act
  1986, s.168);

- when Companies House has been notified that the winding-up is complete (1986 Act, s.205(1)(b));

- if anything else which he considers to be relevant.

The Registry must arrange that the land ceases to be registered as a freehold estate in commonhold land and must take such action as appears appropriate to give effect to determinations made by the liquidator (s.54).

14.31   In this form of winding-up, the association does not become entitled to be registered as proprietor of the units.

Succession order

14.32   A succession order is a way to allow a commonhold to continue, even though the commonhold association has become insolvent, by substituting a new commonhold association (a "phoenix association"). The new, successor, association then takes over the management role and ownership of the common parts.

14.33   The Act gives no direct guidance as to when a succession order is likely to be made. It does, however, tilt the balance in favour of making an order by providing that the court shall grant an application "unless it thinks that the circumstances of the insolvent association make a succession order inappropriate" (s.51(4)). This could be interpreted to mean that there should be a succession order except in a case where the insolvency resulted from the dishonesty or the recklessness of the unit-holders.

14.34   An application for a succession order may be made by the insolvent association, by one of more of its members or by a provisional liquidator (s.51(2)). It must be accompanied by prescribed evidence that a successor commonhold association has been formed and by a certificate given by the directors of the new association that its documents comply with the regulations prescribing the form and contents of memorandum and articles of association of commonhold associations (s.51(3)).

14.35   When the court makes a succession order, the successor commonhold association becomes entitled to be registered as freeholder of the common parts and the insolvent association ceases to be proprietor of them (s.52(1)—(3)). It may make other provisions: dealing with any charge over the common parts, requiring the Land Registry to take action or allowing the liquidator to require the Registry to do so, and making supplementary and incidental provision (s.52(4)).

Where a succession order had been made, the effect of a **14.36** winding-up order is to substitute the successor association for the insolvent association (s.53(2)). The court can order the liquidator to make specified records, or copies, and information available to the successor association (s.53(3), (4)).

Chapter 15

Future changes

15.1 It may, understandably, be thought premature to look to future reforms and amendments to the commonhold legislation before the Act is even in force. However, by looking at experience elsewhere in the World, it is possible to forecast some of the ways in which commonhold is likely to develop. That helps in judging the usefulness of this new system. Also, there are matters which have in effect been left outstanding. They need to be taken into account in any thorough assessment.

Staged development

15.2 The rules which have been initially introduced for commonhold may not conveniently allow a development by stages, even though in practice it may not possible to undertake a major development — involving perhaps a number of subdivided buildings — in any other way. The practicalities of building, connecting to services, finance and marketing may all require that a major scheme be phased.

15.3 At the various stages of the development, different provisions in the commonhold community statement may be appropriate. Take, *e.g.* an estate on which it is proposed to build two blocks each containing 40 flats. Assuming that all flats should make equal contributions to the common-hold association's expenses, when the first block is completed, each flat should pay a service charge contribution of 2.5 per cent. On completion of the second block, this would change to 1.25 per cent. It would not be attractive to require an amendment to the commonhold community statement, particularly if more extensive changes were needed, but neither would it be appropriate to call upon the developer to pay half the expenses during a period when they were only incurred in relation to the occupied half of the property.

If the building period for a commonhold registered without **15.4** unit-holders was lengthy, the transitional period during which the developer had special protection would be extended. This could deter early buyers and prejudice sales. The developer would nevertheless need protection while the later stages of the development were completed.

The answer to these and other problems could be rules **15.5** which would allow a development by stages. Each successive completed part of the final commonhold could be added when it was finished, or possibly when it had been sold. Other jurisdictions have this type of facility, usually added after they have had experience of a basic common-hold system.

Adverse possession and prescription

The Act does not address the relationship between the **15.6** commonhold system and the rules which allow the title to be acquired by adverse possession and the acquisition of easements by prescription. This raises unanswerable questions (para.13.42).

If the squatter acquires title to a whole commonhold unit, **15.7** he is probably entitled to become the unit-holder and to be a member of the commonhold association. Possibly, he is obliged to do so. Certainly, it would not be convenient for him to have the option to withdraw the property from the commonhold. Even if the commonhold could continue without the unit in question, the commonhold community statement would have to be amended. The register would have to be corrected.

15.8   It seems unlikely that a squatter would pay the service charge due to the commonhold association in respect of the occupied unit. It is also unlikely that the association would allow arrears to build for long enough to allow a squatter to acquire title. So, unless the commonhold was one which did not need to collect service charges to fund the association, there will be few circumstances in which a squatter becomes entitled to a whole unit.

15.9   The position is, however, more problematical where only part of a commonhold is acquired. The principle is that a unit is indivisible unless the commonhold association consents to a transfer of part of it (para. 11.17). If one unit-holder acquires part of another's unit, the position can be regularised by an amendment to the commonhold community statement. Perhaps, in the absence of agreement, this is a case for rectification (para. 12.20). But what if the squatter uses the part unit independently: is that part to be made into a new, separate unit? What if the squatter is the owner of adjoining land which is not part of the commonhold, and he occupies the two properties as one: is the land to be taken out of the commonhold?

15.10   There are also difficulties if a squatter acquires a right to some of the common parts. That is equally conceivable. There seems to be no bar against a unit-holder adversely possessing part of the common parts. Although he is a member of the association, which owns the common parts, he is in no special fiduciary position. Equally, the squatter could be an outsider. Is the property to be taken out of the commonhold or will it either be added to an existing unit or made into an additional one?

15.11   Similar questions to those thrown up by squatters arise if someone — whether an insider or an outsider — acquires, by prescription, an easement over part of a unit. Unit-holders are forbidden to create certain interests over part of a unit, unless they have the commonhold association's prior approval.

The sanction against dealings which contravene the Act's rules is that the instrument or agreement is of no effect (s.20(5)). This does not address the case of acquisition by adverse possession or prescription, because in those cases there is nothing in writing. **15.12**

At first glance, it may seem that this is not an urgent problem, because years must elapse before title can be claimed by adverse possession or an easement established by prescription. However, in some circumstances time may have begun to run before the commonhold was set up, so the problem may be immediate. **15.13**

Service charges

It may prove necessary to strengthen the provisions for the collection of service charges by commonhold associations. Full and prompt payment is clearly vital to the efficacy and solvency of associations. A fundamental difference between commonhold and leasehold, which could prevent this, may have to be addressed more directly. **15.14**

The ultimate sanction for an unpaid landlord is to forfeit the lease. This in effect gives the landlord priority over any charges affecting the lease, because the result of forfeiture is to remove the security on which the chargees are relying. To preserve their security, the lessee's mortgagees will therefore have a strong incentive to settle outstanding service charges, while no doubt adding the amount to the debt due to them. **15.15**

Forfeiture is not available to a commonhold association, both because there is no landlord-tenant relationship and also because there is a specific prohibition against a commonhold community statement imposing such a sanction for non-compliance with a duty (s.31(8)). **15.16**

Timeshare

At first sight, commonhold — a form of permanent **15.17**

freehold ownership — would seem to be incompatible with timeshare, where the ownership is essentially transient albeit repeated. A timeshare property is "accommodation ... used or intended to be used ... by a class of persons ... all of whom have rights to use ... that accommodation ... for intermittent periods of short duration" (Timeshare Act 1992, s.1(1)(a)). However, there would be a way in which, with minimal adaptation, commonhold could be usefully used for timeshare developments.

15.18   If a timeshare property is physically of the type which would be suitable for a commonhold, the development will be subject to the same drawbacks as other cases in which commonhold is not used. Difficulties with management and the enforceability of positive obligations mean that leases are used, with all their inherent problems. Other timeshare developments offer participants "club membership", which guarantees their rights as a matter of contract, but generally as licensees without the security of genuine property ownership.

15.19   It would not be possible to have the freehold of timeshare units owned on a rotating basis by a series of people who had bought an entitlement of an annual week or fortnight. But a feasible system would be to vest the ownership of individual units in trustees who held that unit in trust for its various timeshare owners. Such a trust is already possible, but the advantage that commonhold would offer is in the uniform and fully enforceable regulations governing the use of the property.

15.20   The Act already provides for the direct enforcement of regulations by and against tenants of units. A statutory amendment could extend these arrangements to trust beneficiaries entitled to occupy under the terms of the trust. In that way, timeshare could be made at the same time both more secure and better regulated.

Accommodation for the elderly

15.21   Commonhold developments are an ideal way to create sheltered and other residential accommodation for the elderly. They have been extensively used for this purpose in other jurisdictions. The structure for providing and managing communal facilities and services linked to the accommodation is built into the system and while the management is under the ultimate control of the unit-holders, it can be run on a day-to-day basis by professionals.

However, the Act appears to rule out the possibility of requiring prospective unit-holders to satisfy an age qualification (para. 10.3). Appropriate arrangements for the benefit of unit-holders could nevertheless be provided without insisting that unit-holders fall within the class likely to benefit; but that is likely to result eventually in a mixed group of residents and internal dissent about the nature and level of the services provided. Under the present rules this form of development is therefore likely to prove unsatisfactory. **15.22**

There is an active market in providing sheltered and serviced leasehold accommodation for the elderly. The arguments for allowing commonhold to be used for this purpose are the same as the general arguments recommending this form of secure freehold ownership, fortified by the particular need of this group of residents to receive reliable services. **15.23**

RULES IN OTHER JURISDICTIONS

Legislation for systems which are the equivalent to commonhold elsewhere in the World has introduced rules to regulate local concerns. Many are matters which have not so far caused worry in England and Wales. So it is understandable that the Act contains no equivalent provisions and there may be no need to introduce them in the future. It is, nevertheless, useful to outline some of the matters, for future reference if the situation changes. **15.24**

Sales off plan

Contracts for the sale of a unit entered into before it is built can cause difficulties and in some places they are forbidden. In those jurisdictions, the rule is that the whole common-hold must be physically completed before sales are **15.25** negotiated, or sometimes before a sale can be completed. Although, in this country, the extent of each unit must be defined on paper (s.11(2)(b)), a unit can be sold before it physically exists.

15.26 Experience of buying newly developed properties in England and Wales does not suggest that any restriction is needed. But arguably the nature of commonhold developments makes a difference. In the case of a commonhold unit it is particularly important that a buyer has a guarantee that the whole property will be built, not merely the unit which he is buying. Take two examples. The buyer has an interest in ensuring that promised communal facilities are forthcoming; they will probably be provided on the common parts, but may add materially to the value of the unit. Similarly, the percentage of the cost of communal services for which a unit-holder is responsible will depend on the number of other unit-holders who contribute. Unless all the promised units are built, a buyer may find himself with a proportionately greater liability that he expected.

Sweetheart contracts

15.27 Promoters of new developments elsewhere have taken unfair advantage of unit-holders, by making arrangements during the development period which benefit the promoter's associates to the prejudice of the unit-holders. They enter into long-term contracts in the name of (the equivalent of) the commonhold association. The obligations continue to bind the association after the promoter no longer has an interest in the property. The contracts are on terms which unduly favour the associate of the promoter.

15.28 There are many opportunities for this type of malpractice. Two examples can be given. First, the association engages the services of a managing agent connected with the promoter on an extended contract at a high fee rate. Because of the length of the appointment, it is not open to the unit-holders to reconsider it when they take control of the association. Secondly, communal facilities promised to unit-holders — *e.g.* the use of a swimming pool or squash courts — are secured on adjoining property outside the commonhold, under a lease reserving a higher than market rent. The unit-holders have the benefit of the facilities which they were promised, but the burden on the association, and therefore on the service charge, is unreasonably great.

Index